The Best *Little* Grammar Book *Ever!*

Second Edition

More books by Arlene Miller, The Grammar Diva

The Best Little Grammar Book Ever: 101 Ways to Impress With Your Writing and Speaking (First Edition)—paperback and e-book

Correct Me If I'm Wrong: Getting Your Grammar, Punctuation, and Word Usage Right—paperback and e-book

The Great Grammar Cheat Sheet: 50 Grammar, Punctuation, Writing, and Word Usage Tips You Can Use Now—e-book

Beyond Worksheets: Creative Lessons for Teaching Grammar in Middle School and High School—e-book

The Best Grammar Workbook Ever: Grammar, Punctuation, and Word Usage for Ages 10 Through 110—paperback and e-book

Fifty Shades of Grammar: Scintillating and Saucy Sentences, Syntax, and Semantics from The Grammar Diva—paperback and e-book

Coming Soon:

The Best Little Grammar Workbook Ever!

The Best Little Book of Confused Words and Phrases Ever!

If you are the proud owner of any of these books, we always appreciate reviews on Amazon, Goodreads, or your favorite website.

Thank you!

The Best *Little* Grammar Book

EVER!

Speak and Write with Confidence

Second Edition

Arlene Miller

THE GRAMMAR DIVA

bigwords101
Petaluma, California

The Best Little Grammar Book Ever! Speak and Write with Confidence. Avoid Common Mistakes. Second Edition

Cover design by Matt Hinrichs

Interior design and formatting by Marny K. Parkin

Publisher's Cataloging-in-Publication Data

Miller, Arlene. The Best Little Grammar Book Ever! Speak and Write with Confidence. Avoid Common Mistakes. Second Edition, 2016

p. cm. Includes appendixes and index
ISBN 978-0-9911674-4-9

1. English language—Grammar. 2. English language—Usage. 3. English language—Grammar—Self-instruction

Library of Congress: PE 1106.M550
Dewey: 428.2

Published by bigwords101, P.O. Box 4483, Petaluma, CA 94955 USA

website and blog: www.bigwords101.com

Contact Ingram or the publisher for quantity discounts for your company, organization, or educational institution.

To Jake and Shelley
My greatest loves and my inspirations

Contents

Chapter 6
Confusing Things 65

Acknowledgments

It does indeed take at least a village to write and publish a book. And as usual, there are many people to thank—but hopefully, you all know who you are by now, so I will keep this short.

Thank you to my inspirations, who have already been thanked in the dedication: my children, Shelley and Jake; and my son-in-law, Josh. Thank you to my friends: Bobbi Noderer, Frances Caballo, Jeannie Thomas, and Edie Partridge for the love and continuing support.

Thank you to Marny Parkin, my designer; Matt Hinrichs, my cover designer; Gil Namur, my website maven; and John DeGaetano, my business advisor and friend.

Thank you to Grace Bogart and Ray Lawrason from Copperfield's Books, who have been supporting my books from the beginning.

Thank you to my inspirational and helpful colleagues: Linda Reid, Robin Moore, Linda Jay, Jeff Deck, Jeane Slone, Pete Masterson, Sheri Graves, and Joel Friedlander.

And thank you to the rest of you . . . you know who you are.

Introduction

It has been six years since I wrote my first grammar book, the first edition of the book you are currently holding in your hands. Since then, I have written several other grammar books, have begun a grammar blog, and have continued the fight for good grammar!

The language does change, and the standards of our language do evolve—although slowly—so I thought it was time to write a second edition of *The Best Little Grammar Book Ever!* This time there will be an accompanying workbook, *The Best Little Grammar Workbook Ever!* which will be released this year as well.

In addition to including changes in language standards, this new edition is formatted differently and has additions and deletions from the original version. I hope these changes will make the book even more helpful than readers have found the first edition.

You may ask what made me begin to write grammar books in the first place. During my many years as a technical writer, editor, and English teacher, I saw the same errors, questions, and problems come up repeatedly. I decided to put these grammatical issues together in a book that would be friendly and easy to use. Thus, the first edition of this book was born.

Although it does contain a review of grammar, this book is not a grammar textbook, nor is it a complete grammar reference. It is intended to address those issues that are most problematic to people when they write or speak. This book will be helpful to almost anyone who wants to write and speak (and even e-mail) correctly—students from junior high school through college; anyone looking for that first job, a better job, or a new career; career professionals; those whose native language is not English; and just about anyone else who has ever had a question related to grammar or writing.

Arlene Miller, M.A. THE GRAMMAR DIVA

Petaluma, California

How to Use This Book

*T*he *Best Little Grammar Book Ever!* contains both a grammar review (Chapters 1 through 4) and common mistakes and problems in writing and speaking (Chapters 5 through 8). It is neither a complete grammar textbook nor a complete grammar reference; if it were, it would be called *The Best* Big *Grammar Book Ever!* I decided to focus on the topics that cause the most confusion, questions, and errors.

I recommend, therefore, that you first read through the book. After you have read it and know what it contains, you can use it as a reference book whenever you have a question.

The first four chapters of the book present a grammar review. Chapter 1 is about the parts of speech. You probably learned them in grammar school, but maybe you have forgotten some of them. Chapter 2 discusses sentence structure: What is the function of each word in a sentence? What are phrases and clauses? Chapter 3 reviews punctuation, and Chapter 4 provides capitalization standards.

The information contained in these first four chapters is important because the same concepts come up in the later chapters. Do take time to learn any information that is contained in the **Notes** and **Helpful Hints,** which directly affect your writing and speaking.

Chapter 5 begins the discussion of common problems in grammar. In this chapter you will learn some things **not** to do in your writing and speaking. Chapter 6 talks about confusing words—those words that are similar but not the same—and tells you which is which. You will never again confuse *who's* and *whose!* In Chapter 7 you will find some important grammar issues. Chapter 8 contains the finishing touches, for example, how to write numbers and how to capitalize titles. At the end of the book, there is a final test with fifty questions. There are five appendixes: commonly misspelled words, commonly mispronounced words, a writing lesson, a glossary of grammar terms, and the answers to the final test. There is also a complete index.

You are holding this book. You are on your way to becoming a more confident writer and speaker. If you have any comments about this book, or if you have a question about something that is not included here (and you think it should be), please contact me. I can be reached at info@bigwords101.com. Please visit my website at www.bigwords101.com.

Arlene Miller, The Grammar Diva

Conventions Used in This Book

1. I have used *italics* in examples and to indicate words used as themselves.

2. I have used **boldface** to introduce new words.

3. I have used ***boldface italics*** when I really want you to see something!

4. Notes and Helpful Hints are set off with lines.

5. I have used a conversational tone in this book to make it easy to read.

A double negative is a no-no.

—*Author unknown*

Chapter 1

The Basics: Parts of Speech

You may remember hearing about the **parts of speech** way back in elementary school. The parts of speech are simply the categories into which every word in the language fits. These parts of speech are the building blocks of the English (or any) language. When people refer to the parts of speech, they mean the **eight** categories into which all words can be placed. You probably remember terms such as **nouns** and **verbs**, but do you recall all eight parts of speech?

Let me mention two things before we continue:

1. Some words can be used as more than one part of speech. The part of speech depends upon how a word is used in a particular sentence. For example, a word might be used as a noun in one sentence, and the same word might be used as a verb in the next sentence. Of course, this is not true of all words.

2. Is it important to know all the parts of speech? No, not necessarily. However, many times in this book, and in any grammar or writing book or class, the specific parts of speech will be referred to; after all, they are the building blocks upon which the language is built.

Here are the **eight** parts of speech:

1. Noun
2. Pronoun
3. Verb
4. Adjective
5. Adverb
6. Preposition
7. Conjunction
8. Interjection

This chapter briefly discusses these eight parts of speech.

1.1 Nouns

Think back to third grade. Does this sound familiar?

"A noun is a person, place, or thing."

A noun can also be an emotion or idea. Therefore, a noun is a person or a thing of some type, whether or not you can see it.

Here are some nouns:

sun	*California*	*family*
girl	*doctor*	*religion*
dog	*book*	*Susie*
happiness	*rain*	*seashore*

The words above are all people, places, things, ideas, or emotions.

• People: Susie, girl, doctor, family

• Places: California, seashore

• Things: dog, book, sun, rain

• Ideas or emotions: happiness, religion

Helpful Hint! How can you check to see if a word is being used as a noun? Usually, you can put the words *a, an,* or *the* before nouns. Note that most words that begin with capital letters are nouns:

the sun, a girl, a dog, a religion, the Empire State Building

---

The Five Types of Nouns

There are five categories of nouns:

1. **Common nouns** are regular nouns that do not start with capital letters, such as *happiness, boy, desk,* and *city.*

2. **Proper nouns** start with a capital letter. They are specific people, places, things, or ideas such as *Florida, Buddhism, Joe,* and *Thanksgiving.*

3. **Concrete nouns** represent things you can see, hear, smell, taste, or feel. Most nouns are concrete. Concrete nouns are either common or proper too. Concrete nouns include *grass, paper, perfume, air* (you can feel it), *Susie,* and *Golden Gate Bridge.*

4. **Abstract nouns** represent ideas or emotions; you cannot perceive them with any of your senses. Abstract nouns are either common or proper too. *Religion, happiness, anger,* and *Buddhism* fall into this category.

5. **Collective nouns** represent a group of things or people without being plural (although they can also be made plural). *Family, group, orchestra, audience, flock, bunch,* and *herd* fall into this category. These nouns become important when we discuss noun and verb agreement in Chapter 7.1.

To summarize, every noun is either proper or common, and either concrete or abstract. For example, *girl* is common and concrete. And the *Theory of Relativity* is proper and abstract.

1.2 Pronouns

A pronoun takes the place of a noun. For example, instead of saying

Sally brought Sally's books back to the library.

You say

*Sally brought **her** books back to the library. Her* is a pronoun. *Sally* is called the **antecedent.** (The antecedent is the word that the pronoun replaces.)

Some common pronouns are *I, you, he, she, them, they, we, us, him, her,* and *it.*

Helpful Hint! When you write, make sure that it is always clear to what or whom your pronoun refers.

Types of Pronouns

There are six types of pronouns.

1. **Personal pronouns** are the common pronouns that are listed above, such as *I, me, you, he, she, it, they, her,* and *him.*

    *I bought a new hat, but **I** lost **it** somewhere. (It* refers to *hat.)*

2. **Demonstrative pronouns** point things out. There are only four of them: *this, that, these,* and *those.*

    ***This** is my new CD. (This* refers to *CD.)*

3   **Interrogative pronouns** are used to ask questions. There are five of them: *which, who, whose, whom,* and *what.*

    ***Who** is that man?*

4. **Relative pronouns** begin adjective clauses (more about that later). There are five of them: *which, whom, whose, who,* and *that.* Notice that they are almost the same as the interrogative pronouns. However, relative pronouns do not ask a question, and they do not appear at the beginning of a sentence. Here are some examples of how they are used.

    *My neighbor, **who** is a lawyer, just came back from Paris.*

    *You can borrow the book **that** I just finished.*

5. **Reflexive/intensive pronouns** are the ones with *-self* at the end. Here are some examples:

    *I baked that cake **myself**. (Used as a reflexive: myself* reflects back to *I.)*

    I **myself** baked that cake. (Used as an intensive: *myself* emphasizes *I.)*

Helpful Hint! Do not use the *-self* pronouns any other way. It is incorrect to say, "He gave the book to *myself*." It is correct to say, "He gave the book to *me*." And never begin a sentence with a *-self* pronoun.

6. Indefinite pronouns include *someone, everyone, anyone, no one, some-body, anybody, everybody, everything, something, anything, nothing, none, few, many, several, all, some,* and many more. They are important because you need to know which ones are singular and which ones are plural, so you know which verb and personal pronoun to use with them.

Big Issue: The Singular *They*

Someone, everyone, anyone, no one, everybody, nobody, anybody, somebody, something, everything, anything, nothing, each, either, and *neither* are some common **indefinite pronouns** that are singular. They always use a singular verb (for example, *is* rather than *are*). However, there is sometimes another pronoun in the sentence that refers back to this indefinite pronoun. Sometimes we don't know whether the indefinite pronoun—for example, *every-one* or *somebody*—refers to a male or female. So do we use *he* or do we use *she* to refer back to *everyone,* for example? Generally, we would use the bulky construction of *he or she.* In the past, just *he* was used to represent males and females, but this is no longer acceptable. Other things that were tried were alternating between *he* and *she,* which is obviously confusing. And *he/she* is not really acceptable in writing. So, if you don't want to use *he or she,* which is perfectly acceptable, you have two other choices:

1. Use the plural pronoun *they* as a singular, which is now acceptable.
2. Rewrite the sentence to avoid the problem. This is my choice and can usually be done quite easily.

Here are some examples to illustrate this grammatical issue:

*Everyone is bringing **his or her** own lunch to the picnic.* (*Everyone* is singular. The verb *is bringing* is singular, and the pronoun *his or her* is singular. They all agree, and this sentence is technically grammatically correct.)

*Everyone is bringing **their** own lunch to the picnic.* Here, *their* is being used as a singular. Even though *their* refers back to the singular *every-one, their* is technically plural. However, you can now use this construction if you want. I don't personally like it, and I prefer to rewrite the sentence.

Everyone is bringing lunch to the picnic. (rewrite)

We are all bringing lunches to the picnic. (different rewrite)

All the people are bringing their own lunches to the picnic. (yet another rewrite)

Some, but not as many, of the indefinite pronouns are plural: *all, several, few, many*

> *Several are bringing their own lunches to the picnic.* (*Several* is plural. The verb *are bringing* is plural, and the pronoun *their* is plural. Correctly, they all match.)

Helpful Hint! How can you tell whether a verb is singular or plural? Use the verb with the pronoun *he* (which is singular), and whichever verb form sounds right is the singular form. Then, use the verb with the pronoun *they* (which is plural), and whichever verb form you use is the plural form.

> *He **walks** home.* (*Walks* is the singular verb form.)

> *They **walk** home.* (*Walk* is the plural verb form.)

Another Helpful Hint! Do not confuse **pronouns** with **proper nouns**. Proper nouns begin with capital letters and are nouns (person, place, thing, idea). Pronouns are a different part of speech, and they stand in for nouns.

> Proper Nouns: *New York, Henry, Catholicism, Italy, Red Cross*

> Pronouns: *she, anyone, they, which*

1.3 Verbs

Verb: It's what you do! Verbs are action words. *Jump, run, bake, read, swim, give,* and *walk* are examples of verbs.

Verbs can also indicate **mental** action, not just **physical** action. *Think, wonder, plan,* and *consider* are also verbs.

*The boys **hid** in the forest.* (*Hid* is a verb.)

*I **took** the math test yesterday.* (*Took* is a verb.)

*The hotel **provided** us with rooms after the game.* (*Provided* is a verb.)

Helpful Hint! Every sentence needs a verb. Without a verb, there is no sentence.

Linking Verbs

There is another important type of verb called a **linking verb**. A linking verb ties together the word or words before the verb and the word or words after the verb. The linking verb is like the equal sign in math. The most common linking verb is the verb *to be*. That verb has many different forms. You probably recognize the *to be* verb by these familiar forms: *is, am, are, will be, was, has been, have been,* etc. Here are some linking verbs "in action":

*I **am** hungry.* (*Hungry* describes *I*; they are linked by the verb *am*.)

*She **was** a dancer.* (*Dancer* describes *she*; they are linked by the verb *was*.)

There are linking verbs other than *to be* and its various forms. *Taste, appear, look, become,* and *feel* are also linking verbs. Usually, if you can substitute a form of the *to be* verb and the sentence still makes sense, you have a linking verb. Linking verbs are often verbs of the senses.

*She **felt** tired today.* (*Tired* describes *she*; they are linked by the verb *felt*. She **is** tired today makes sense.)*

*He **became** angry at me.* (*Angry* describes *he*; they are linked by the verb *became*. He **was** angry at me makes sense.)

Mary threw the ball. (*Ball* does not describe *Mary*, so we know *threw* is **not** a linking verb. *Mary **is** the ball* makes no sense.)

To make things just a bit more confusing, words like *taste, smell, look,* and *feel* are sometimes linking verbs and sometimes action verbs. Notice the difference:

*The cake **tasted** great!* (*Great* describes *cake*; *tasted* is a linking verb. The cake didn't do anything. And it has no tongue to taste anything! There is no action here.)

*I **tasted** the cake.* (*Cake* does not describe *I*; *taste* is an action verb here.)

Note: Why does it matter which verbs are linking and which are action? Good question! Usually it doesn't. Sometimes it becomes important to know because it may determine whether you use *I* or *me*, *him* or *he*, *she* or *her*, etc. But more about that later.

Tense

Verbs have some qualities you should know about. One of these is **tense**, which has to do with time. The tense of a verb tells you *when* the action took place. Verbs are the only action part of speech, and they can take place in the past, in the present, or in the future. There are six main tenses, each representing a different time. Each of the six tenses has a partner (the **progressive,** or **continuous,** form), making the total number of tenses twelve. Here they are, using the action verb *walk*:

1. Present tense: *I walk to the store.* (It is happening now.)

    Present progressive tense: *I am walking to the store.*

2. Past tense: *I walked to the store.* (It happened in the past, and it is over.)

    Past progressive: *I was walking to the store.*

3. Future tense: *I will walk to the store.* (It will happen in the future. Please don't bother using *shall* unless you are talking about a legal agreement.)

    Future progressive: *I will be walking to the store.*

4. Present perfect: *I have walked to the store every day this week.* (Uses *have or has*. It happened in the past and is likely continuing.)

    Present perfect progressive: *I have been walking to the store.*

5. Past perfect: *Seven runners had already finished the race by the time I crossed the finish line.* (Uses *had*. It happened in the past by the time something else happened in the past.)

   Past perfect progressive: *I had been running for three hours before I crossed the finish line.*

6. Future perfect tense*: I will have played piano for ten years by the time I graduate from high school.* (It will happen in the future before some other future event.)

   Future perfect progressive: *I will have been playing piano for ten years by the time I graduate from high school.*

Notice that the **progressive tenses** use the *-ing* ending. A significant difference between these two tense forms is that we use the **simple present tense** for things that are permanent or exist in general and the **present progressive tense** for things that may change or are temporary.

You can probably figure out when to use the tenses. Here are some guidelines:

1. Do not switch tenses without a reason. For example, "*I go to the movies, and I saw my cousin there,*" is incorrect because the tense switches from present to past, when both things actually happened at the same time.

2. Don't use the present tense for something that happened in the past. For example, "*I go to the movies, and I see my cousin there.*" Since this happened in the past, say, "*I went to the movies, and I saw my cousin there.*"

3. When you talk about things that happened in a book you read or a movie you saw, generally use the present tense. It is more interesting— and the book or movie is still there, so it didn't really happen in the past, although the reading did! For example: "*I just **read** Romeo and Juliet. It **is** a story in which two young lovers **are** from warring families and it **ends** very sadly.*" (*Read* is in the past tense, but the verbs in the accounting of the story are all present tense.)

Note: Notice the words used with the verb *walk* in some of the tenses. Although they look like forms of the linking verb *to be*, they are not. Because they are used with another verb (in this case, *walk*), they are called **helping verbs**. For example, in "*I **will have been** walking*," *will have been* are helping verbs, and *walking* is the main verb. If *will have been* is used without a main verb, *will* and *have* are linking verbs and *been* is the main verb. For example, in "*I will have been a teacher for three years . . .*" *will* and *have* are helping verbs and *been* is the main verb. There is no other verb in the sentence, and *teacher* describes *I*. The verb and its helping verbs (if there are any) are called a **verb phrase**.

Here are the tenses for the verb *to be*, using the pronoun *you*:

- Present/Present Progressive: you are/you are being
- Past/Past Progressive: you were/you were being
- Future/Future Progressive: you will be/you will be being
- Present Perfect/Present Perfect Progressive: you have been/you have been being
- Past Perfect/Past Perfect Progressive: you had been/you had been being
- Future Perfect/Future Perfect Progressive: you will have been/you will have been being

---

Note: Some verbs have irregular forms that you just have to memorize.

Walk is regular because the past tense simply adds *-ed*. However, look at these verbs:

I *swim*, but I *swam*, and I have *swum*.

She *eats*, but she *ate*, and she has *eaten*.

I *bring*, but I *brought*, and I have *brought* (not *brang* or *brung* or *broughten*!)

Refer to Chapter 7.9 for some common irregular verb forms.

Voice

Another quality of verbs besides tense is **voice**. There are two voices: **active** and **passive**. In **active** voice, the **subject** of the sentence (usually the noun or pronoun before the verb) is doing the action. Can you see the difference between the voices?

>   *He drove to the mall.* (**active**–the subject of the sentence, *he*, did the driving.)

>   *He was driven to the mall by his sister.* (**passive**)

When you write, use active voice most of the time. It is stronger and more effective. See more about this in Chapter 7.5.

Transitive/Intransitive

Another thing about verbs—yes, they are rather complicated! Verbs are also classified as either **transitive** or **intransitive**. The dictionary refers to verbs as either **vi** (verb intransitive) or **vt** (verb transitive) where it tells you the part of speech.

Transitive verbs have a direct object; intransitive verbs don't. Sometimes a verb can be both, depending on how it is being used in that particular sentence. Direct objects are discussed in Chapter 2.3. Simply put, if you ask *what* or *who* about the verb, the answer is the direct object. Here are some examples.

>   *They played baseball.* (Played what? Baseball. *Baseball* is the direct object, and *played* is transitive.)

>   *They played in the yard.* (Played what or who? The sentence does not tell you. There is no direct object, and *played* is intransitive.)

Helpful Hint! Is it important to know if a verb is transitive or intransitive? Sometimes. There are some verbs that are confusing, and the verb form you use depends upon whether it is transitive or intransitive.

>   *He lies in the sun.* (The verb is intransitive. Use *lie*.)

>   *He lays his hat on the table.* (The verb is transitive. Use *lay*. And more about *lay* and *lie* in Chapter 6.13.)

Another Helpful Hint! You already learned in Chapter 1.1 that you can tell if a word is a noun by putting *a, an,* or *the* in front of it. How can you tell if a word is a verb? Put the word *to* in front of it: *to jump, to think, to be, to study, to allow.*

Mood

As if we haven't already discussed enough characteristics of verbs, they also have **mood.** No, not moods like happy, sad, or angry. The moods of verbs are **indicative, imperative,** and **subjunctive.**

Indicative mood is simply a statement, and is the most common mood. Imperative mood is used for a command. You don't need to worry about either of those. **Subjunctive** is the tricky one.

Subjunctive mood is sometimes used correctly without even a thought. However, there are times when it should be used and isn't: When something is not true or is a wish, use subjunctive. Here are some examples of subjunctive:

> *If I **were** rich, I would buy a house by the ocean.* (I am not rich, so I use *were* instead of *If I was rich.*)

> *I wish I **were** rich, so I could build a house by the ocean.* (Usually subjunctive is used with *wish.* I don't say *I wish I was rich.*)

1.4 Adjectives

Adjectives are pretty simple. They are used to describe nouns (people, places, things, ideas) and sometimes pronouns. Adjectives can also describe other adjectives. They tell **how many, what kind,** or **which ones.** Here are some examples of adjectives describing (or **modifying**) nouns:

> ***Pretty*** bird, ***six*** trees, ***blue*** dress, ***handsome*** Harry, ***good*** idea

Here is an example of an adjective that describes a pronoun: *He is **handsome.*** Notice that the structure is a little different here. When describing a pronoun, the adjective is usually **after** the verb rather than right before the pronoun. Notice that in this type of sentence, the verb is **always** a linking verb (*is,* in this sentence).

Here is an adjective describing another adjective: *bright blue* dress. The adjective *blue* is describing the noun *dress*; the adjective *bright* is describing the type of *blue* (not the dress).

What if you said *new blue dress*? *New* and *blue* are both adjectives, but they both describe the noun *dress.* It is a *new* dress, and it is a *blue* dress. It is not the *blue* that is *new.*

When both adjectives describe the noun (as in *new blue dress*), you may need a comma between the two adjectives. If you can put the word *and* between the two adjectives, and the phrase makes sense, use a comma.

> *That is an old, torn shirt!* (*old and torn* makes sense; use comma)

> *That is a pretty pink shirt.* (*pretty and pink* shirt doesn't sound right; no comma)

Other Types of Adjectives

There are a couple of special types of adjectives. However, they have the same function as any other adjective.

1. **Demonstrative:** In Chapter 1.2 we discussed demonstrative pronouns. They are *this, that, these,* and *those.* These same four words, when placed right before a noun, are demonstrative adjectives. Notice the difference:

   This *is my book.* (demonstrative pronoun)

   This *book is mine.* (demonstrative adjective describing *book*)

2. **Proper:** Proper adjectives are just like proper nouns; they begin with a capital letter. Here are a few examples: ***Thanksgiving*** *dinner,* ***Italian*** *food,* ***Catholic*** *religion*

Notes:

1. Some words can be used as more than one part of speech, depending on how they are used in that particular sentence. Nouns can often be used as adjectives. Here are some examples: *beef stew, bread pudding, prom dress, Christmas vacation.*

2. The words *a, an,* and *the* are called **articles**. Sometimes they are thought of as a separate part of speech, but they are really adjectives.

1.5 Adverbs

Like adjectives, adverbs are **describing words**. Adverbs are used to describe verbs (action words). Sometimes adverbs also describe adjectives or other adverbs. Adverbs tell **where, when,** and **how.** Adverbs usually end in *-ly,* but not always.

She ran *quickly. Quickly* describes how she *ran. (Ran* is the verb.)

He is *extremely* intelligent. (Here, *extremely* describes the adjective *intelligent.)*

He writes *really* quickly. (*Really* is an adverb that describes *quickly,* also an adverb. *Quickly* describes **how** he *writes. Writes* is the verb.)

Note that some words ending in *-ly* are not adverbs at all; they are adjectives because they describe nouns. Here are some examples:

What a *lovely* dress. (*Lovely* describes the noun *dress,* so it is an adjective.)

I have three sisters, so I am never *lonely.* (*Lonely* describes the pronoun *I.* The two words are connected with the linking verb *am.* Note that the word *never* is an adverb telling *when.* It describes the adjective *lonely.)*

Many adverbs do not end in *-ly.* Some of these adverbs include *now, then, soon, very, only, often,* and *not.*

Flat Adverbs

Most adverbs that end in *-ly* are adjectives when the *-ly* is dropped. For example, *slow* is an adjective, and *slowly* is an adverb:

He has a *slow* car. *(Slow* is an adjective describing *car*.)

He drives *slowly*. *(Slowly* is an adverb describing how he *drives*.)

He drives *slow*. *(Slow* is a **flat adverb** because it is an adjectival form, but is being used as an adverb here. Avoid using flat adverbs.)

See more about flat adverbs in Chapter 5.11.

Helpful Hints!

1. There is usually more than one place to put an adverb in a sentence. Sometimes the location of an adverb changes the meaning of a sentence. (See Chapter 6.16 for a discussion about the adverb *only*.) Other times, the sentence is simply clearer if you place the adverb close to the verb.

   I *go* for a walk in the woods *often*.

   I *often go* for a walk in the woods. (better way to write it)

2. Be careful not to overuse the adverbs *really* and *very*. Avoid using two *really*s or *very*s in a row. (example: *really, really* cold)

1.6 Prepositions

Prepositions are usually (but not always) little words, and they are always part of a phrase (a group of a few related words) known, not surprisingly, as a **prepositional phrase**. A prepositional phrase generally consists of (1) a **preposition**, (2) sometimes an **article** (*a, an,* or *the*), and (3) a **noun** or **pronoun** (which is called the **object of the preposition**). Prepositional phrases usually answer the questions where? or when?

Here are some examples of prepositions in a phrase (the preposition is in *italics*):

in the box	*down* the stairs
with my friends	*beside* the desk
at the store	*within* the city
out of the room	*for* the committee
of mine	*among* the students
between them	*beneath* the table
by me	*after* the storm
to the movies	*before* his speech
up the tree	*along* the riverbank

There are many other prepositions, but you get the idea.

If a preposition does not have a noun or pronoun after it, it is **not** a preposition; it is an adverb.

I am going *inside the house.* (prepositional phrase; *inside* is a preposition.)

I am going *inside.* (There is no prepositional phrase; *inside* is an adverb here.)

Helpful Hints!

1. There is an old "rule" that says *never end a sentence with a preposition.* That "rule" is pretty much gone now. Most of the time it is fine to end a sentence with a preposition. However, you don't want to end a sentence with the preposition *at* or with a preposition that is not needed in the sentence at all.

    Wrong: *Where are you **at**?*   **Right:** *Where are you?*

    Wrong: *Where are you going **to**?*   **Right:** *Where are you going?*

    Fine to say: *Whom are you going with?* **OR** *With whom are you going?* (The first question ends with the preposition *with*, and it is fine, although I prefer the second option of starting the sentence with the preposition.

2. It is important to be able to recognize prepositional phrases. Often, recognizing a prepositional phrase will help you decide whether to use *who* or *whom*, *I* or *me*, *him* or *he*, etc. We will talk about this in Chapter 6.10.

1.7 Conjunctions

Conjunctions join things. They join words, phrases (a short group of related words), and even sentences together. (See Chapter 2.5 for information about phrases.) The most common conjunction is *and*.

*Jack **and** Jill* (joins two words together)

*I went to school **and** to the movies.* (joins two phrases together)

*I am a student, **and** my brother is a dentist.* (joins two sentences together)

And is called a **coordinating conjunction**. There are seven coordinating conjunctions. They are *for, and, nor, but, or, yet,* and *so.* The first letters of these words spell **FANBOYS**.

Remember the "word" **FANBOYS,** and you will remember these conjunctions!

Subordinating Conjunctions

The **FANBOYS** conjunctions are called **coordinating conjunctions** because they connect, or join, two or more things. There is another kind of conjunction called a **subordinating conjunction**. These conjunctions begin **subordinate clauses** (see Chapter 2.6), even though they may look as if they are joining parts of a sentence.

Subordinating conjunctions include (but are not limited to) these words: *although, since, if, because, until, when,* and *whenever.* Here are some examples illustrating subordinating clauses in sentences:

Although I am small, I am strong. (Subordinate clause begins with *although*.)

Because I have no money, I cannot go to the movies. (Subordinate clause begins with *because*.)

I cannot get my license until I turn sixteen. (Subordinate clause begins with *until*.)

Helpful Hints!

1. When you are joining two things, there is no comma. However, in a series of more than two things, you can use a comma before a*nd*.

I packed shoes and socks.

I packed shoes, socks, and shirts. (The comma before *and* is usually optional and is called the **Oxford**, or series, comma. Refer to Chapter 3.2.)

2. There is generally a comma before a FANBOYS conjunction that connects two sentences.

I sprained my ankle, so I cannot go hiking today.

I cannot go with you, but my sister can.

3. In more formal writing, you probably want to avoid starting sentences with a FANBOYS conjunction. However, beginning a sentence with a conjunction in less formal writing is acceptable now. (See Chapter 8.5.)

1.8 Interjections

Wow! This is an easy part of speech. Interjections are words that don't have a grammatical function in a sentence; they are usually exclamatory words, but not always. Sometimes they are followed by an exclamation point; other times, they are connected to the sentence with a comma.

Here are some interjections: *hey, gosh, ouch, gee whiz, wow,* oh, *well*

Wow! What a nice car!

Ouch! That really hurt!

Well, I think I am going with you.

Oh, I didn't know that.

Even if you do learn to speak correct English,
whom are you going to speak it to?

—Clarence Darrow
US defense lawyer (1857–1938)

Chapter 2

The Basics:
Sentence Structure

Words are combined to make up sentences. A sentence is a complete thought. Almost everything you read is made up of sentences. Every word in a sentence is, of course, one of the eight parts of speech. A sentence might contain more than one instance of a certain part of speech (for example, four nouns or three verbs or five adjectives) and does not need to contain all the parts of speech. In fact, hardly any sentence would contain all eight parts of speech. Besides being one of the parts of speech, each word in a sentence also performs a certain function in the sentence, sometimes as part of a group of words. These functions will be described in this chapter. The function a word performs in the sentence is not necessarily the same as its part of speech. **Parts of speech** refers only to these eight words: *noun, pronoun, verb, adjective, adverb, preposition, conjunction,* and *interjection.*

Every sentence needs a **subject** and a **verb**, but most sentences have additional words.

2.1 Subjects

The subject of a sentence is **always** a noun or a pronoun (or a group of words that functions as a noun), although it is not always a person. It is usually whatever or whoever is doing the action of the verb. The subject is often the first word in a sentence, but not always. Every sentence needs a subject. To find the subject, first find the verb and ask who is doing the action. Some sentences have more than one subject. Here are some examples of subjects:

1. *The **man** tied his shoes.* (The subject is *man.*)
2. ***Everyone** is going to the movies.* (The subject is *everyone.*)
3. ***Who** is knocking at the door?* (The subject is *who.*)
4. *After school, **she** and **I** always do our homework.* (The subject is *she and I*; more than one subject is called a **compound** subject.)
5. *Do **you** know who is at the door?* (The subject is *you.*)
6. ***Jenny** is going to school, and her **brother** is working.* (*Jenny* and *brother* are both subjects.)

2.2 Predicates

The **predicate** of the sentence is the verb. The verb, along with its helping verbs (refer back to Chapter 1.3), is called the **simple predicate**. Every sentence needs at least one verb.

In the examples in Chapter 2.1, the predicates are 1. *tied*, 2. *is going*, 3. *is knocking*, 4. *do*, 5. *know*, 6. *is going* and *is working.*

Note: The **complete predicate** consists of the entire sentence without the **complete subject**. The complete subject is the subject and all the words that go with it. Here is a sentence divided into complete subject and complete predicate:

The small dog in the kitchen (subject)/ is eating the candy, which isn't healthy for dogs. (predicate)

2.3 Objects

There are three types of objects you might find in a sentence: **direct, indirect,** and **objects of prepositions** (refer back to Chapter 1.6). A sentence does not need any objects at all. **A sentence needs only a subject and a verb to make it complete.**

A sentence might have no objects at all, or it might have any combination of the three types of objects. Objects, like subjects, are always nouns or pronouns. Direct objects receive the action of the verb. If you ask *what?* or *who?* after the verb, you will find the direct object.

Indirect objects come between the verb and the direct object. You cannot have an indirect object without a direct object, but you can have a direct object without an indirect object. Examples will help here:

*I threw the **ball** at **James**.* (The direct object is *ball—threw what? James* is the object of the preposition *at.*)

*Jane ate three **pieces** of cake.* (The direct object is *pieces,* not *cake—ate what? Cake* is the object of the preposition *of.*)

*I gave **her** a **gift**.* (*Gift* is the direct object—*gave what?* The indirect object is *her.*)

*Mom baked **me** a **cake**.* (The direct object is *cake—baked what?* The indirect object is *me.*)

2.4 Predicate Words

Linking verbs (refer back to Chapter 1.3) do not have objects: instead, they have **predicate adjectives** and **predicate nominatives** (nouns).

*I am a **writer**.* (*Am* is a linking verb, so *writer* is not an object. Since *writer* is a noun, it is called a **predicate nominative**.)

*I am **happy**.* (*Am* is a linking verb, so there is no object. Since *happy* is an adjective, it is called a **predicate adjective**.)

Note: **Linking** verbs connect the words before and after them. They function as "equal" signs in a sentence; the subject and the predicate word are equal. In the above examples, *I* is the "same" as *writer* and *happy*.

When there is an **action** verb, there is no linking of words before and after the verb. In the sentence *I threw the ball, threw* is not linking *I* and *ball*. *I* am not equal to *ball*!

2.5 Phrases

A phrase is simply a small group of words that go together. It is never a complete sentence, and it never has both a subject and a verb. Phrases add information and variety to your writing. In Chapter 1.3 we discussed **verb phrases** (the verb and its helping verbs).

A phrase functions as a specific part of speech, even if the phrase itself doesn't contain that part of speech at all. For example, prepositional phrases contain prepositions and nouns or pronouns (and sometimes adjectives). And these phrases generally function as either adjectives or adverbs in the sentence.

Here are some common types of phrases:

1. **Prepositional phrases** tell *where* or *when* and contain a preposition and its object (a noun or a pronoun) and sometimes an article and/or an adjective:

   I put it **on the table**. (tells where, so it is an adverb phrase)

   During the movie *the baby cried.* (tells when, so it is an adverb phrase)

   I love that dress **with the blue stripes**. (tells what kind of dress, so it is an adjective phrase)

2. **Infinitive phrases** consist of the word *to* followed by a verb (*to* followed by a verb is called an *infinitive*) and then possibly some other words. This type of phrase is called a **verbal**, since it is made up of a verb form. (Note that *to* is not a preposition here because it is followed by a verb, not an object.) Infinitive phrases function as nouns:

*I want **to go** home now.* (I want what? The phrase is the direct object of the verb *want.*)

***To be a doctor** is my goal.* (What is my goal? This phrase is the subject of the sentence.)

3. **Participial phrases** contain a participle, which is a form of a verb used as an adjective. They usually end in *-ing* or are a past tense form. This type of phrase is also called a verbal, since it contains a verb form.

   ***Running quickly**, I got to school late anyway.* (The phrase describes *I.*)

   *Dad, **driving the car,** wasn't listening.* (The phrase describes *dad.*)

   *I looked at the **newly built** school.* (The phrase describes *school.*)

4. **Appositive phrases** add information to a noun or pronoun and are sometimes set off with commas. They function as adjectives, describing the noun that comes before them.

   *Ann, **my neighbor**, is from Florida.*

   *Ben, **my oldest brother**, is in college.*

Helpful Hints:

Why are phrases important?

1. If you put your phrase in the wrong place in the sentence instead of next to what it describes, you could have a silly sentence. See Chapter 7.3.

2. Especially with appositives, you need to know when to put commas around your phrase and when not to. In general, put commas around your appositive phrase when it doesn't affect the meaning of the sentence and could be left out:

   My oldest sister, Jane, is away at college. (You don't really need her name since you specify she is your oldest sister, and you have just one older sister.)

   My sister Jane is away at college. (No commas because you are telling which sister and implying you have more than one sister.)

2.6 Clauses

A clause, like a phrase, is a group of words. However, a clause has both a subject and a verb. There are two main kinds of clauses, **subordinate** (or **dependent**) and **independent**. An **independent** clause is the same as a sentence, so we don't need to worry about those. A **subordinate** clause, however, is not a complete sentence, so make sure you don't write one and call it a sentence. There are three types of **subordinate** clauses: **adverb, adjective,** and **noun**. Adjective clauses, like adjectives, describe nouns; and adverb clauses describe verbs.

1. **Adjective clauses** always start with the words *who, which, that, whom,* or *whose* (relative pronouns). They never begin a sentence.

    *John, **who is my neighbor,** is on vacation.* (*Who* is the subject of the clause, and *is* is the verb. The clause describes *John.*)

    *The dress **that I bought** is in my closet.* (*I* is the subject of the clause, and *bought* is the verb. The clause describes *the dress.*)

2. **Adverb clauses** start with words such as *if, when, although, because, whenever,* and *since* (subordinating conjunctions, discussed in Chapter 1.7). These clauses can be either at the beginning, middle, or the end of a sentence.

    Because I was late, *I missed the bus.*

    *I missed the bus **because I was late.***

    Although I can cook, *I cannot bake well.*

3. **Noun clauses** act as subjects or objects, just like nouns.

    *I don't know **who you are.*** (Clause is the direct object.)

    Whomever you invite *is fine with me.* (Clause is the subject.)

Notes:

1. When you take an adverb or adjective clause out of the sentence, you still have a complete sentence left.

2. Notice that there is usually no comma before ***because*** (and the other subordinating conjunctions) when the clause is at the end of the sentence. When you put the clause at the beginning of the sentence, you do use a comma.

2.7 Types of Sentences

There are four types of sentences:

1. **Declarative sentences** are statements:

    I went to the basketball game yesterday.

2. **Interrogative sentences** are questions:

    Which teams played yesterday?

3. **Imperative sentences** are commands:

    Let me know next time you go to the game.

4. **Exclamatory sentences** express excitement:

    I just got tickets for the World Series!

Note: Usually, there is no stated subject in a command. The command generally begins with a verb, for example, "Clean your room." The command actually means "You clean your room." The subject of any command is *you*, but it usually does not appear in the sentence.

2.8 Sentence Structures

All sentences are made up of one or more clauses. Remember that a clause is a group of words that has a subject and a verb. Some clauses (independent) are complete sentences and can stand on their own. Other clauses (subordinate) cannot stand on their own; they are not complete thoughts, and they must be added to an independent clause; every sentence needs to include at least one independent clause. Here are the four sentence structures:

Simple Sentence

A simple sentence is **one independent clause**. Here are some simple sentences:

Jack and Jill went up the hill.

I tend to sleep more in the winter than in the summer. (Although this sentence is fancier and has some prepositional phrases, it has only one clause.)

Compound Sentence

A compound sentence contains **two or more simple sentences** (or independent clauses) joined by one of the FANBOYS conjunctions (*for, and, nor, but, or, yet,* and *so*) or a semicolon. Here are some compound sentences:

<u>*I ate my dinner,*</u> *and* <u>*I went to bed.*</u> Notice how both the underlined sections is a sentence all by itself.

<u>*The dog ate the sofa,*</u> <u>*the cat tore the curtains,*</u> *and* <u>*the bird threw seeds everywhere.*</u> (There are three independent clauses in this compound sentence.)

Complex Sentence

A complex sentence contains an independent clause and one or more subordinate (usually adverb or adjective) clauses.

<u>*Because I was late,*</u> *they left without me.* (The subordinate clause is underlined. The other clause is a complete sentence: *They left without me.*)

The woman <u>*who was eating pizza*</u> *spilled her coffee all over me.* (The adjective clause is in the middle of the sentence. The independent clause is *the woman spilled her coffee all over me,* a complete sentence on its own.)

Compound-Complex Sentence

Compound-complex sentences contain two or more independent clauses (compound sentence) and at least one dependent clause: a combination of the complex and compound sentences.

> *I ate my pizza, which was getting cold, and I drank my juice.* The two independent clauses are underlined. The dependent adjective clause is in the middle.

2.9 Not a Sentence: Fragments and Run-Ons

One of the most important things to know when you are writing is the difference between a sentence, a fragment, and a run-on. You must write in complete sentences and avoid run-on sentences and fragments. Run-ons and fragments are grammatically incorrect. Can you ever use a fragment or a run-on sentence? For right now, the answer is **no**. But see Chapter 8.6 for more information about this.

A sentence is a complete thought. It can be really short or really long. However, all it really needs is a subject and a verb. Here are some examples of sentences:

1. *He ran.*
2. *He ran and ran and ran and ran and ran and ran and ran, and then he stopped.* (No, it's not a run-on just because it seems to run on and on!)
3. *Because I have no money, I cannot travel this year.*

Fragments

A sentence fragment is not a sentence, but sometimes people think it is. A fragment is not a complete thought. Sometimes people write a subordinate clause and think it is a sentence, but it isn't. Here are some samples of fragments.

1. *Because I have no money.* (What about if you had no money? This is **not** a complete thought. It is fine to add it to a sentence, as shown in sentence example #3 above, but it cannot stand on its own.)

2. *And I went with my friend.* (Generally, we do not begin a sentence with *and, so, but,* or *or*. However, refer to Chapter 8.5 for more information about this.)

3. *If I try really hard.* (This is another subordinate clause that cannot stand on its own.)

Run-Ons

A run-on sentence is another writing mistake. Here is a run-on:

We went to the movies, our friends went to the museum.

A run-on contains more than one complete sentence without proper punctuation. Two complete thoughts (sentences) can correctly be separated in one of these three ways:

1. Put a period between them, and start the second one with a capital letter.

   We went to the movies. Our friends went to the museum.

2. Put a semicolon between them if the two sentences are closely related.

   We went to the movies; our friends went to the museum.

3. Put a FANBOYS conjunction (*for, and, nor, but, or, yet, so*) between them.

   We went to the movies, and our friends went to the museum. (Use a comma before the conjunction unless the sentence is very short.)

Note: Do not ever separate two complete sentences with just a comma! That is a run-on (called a comma splice). It is incorrect.

2.10 Sentence Variety Patterns

Sentence variety means structuring your sentences in different ways to make your writing more interesting. For example, instead of using all simple sentences (see Chapter 2.8) and putting the subject at the beginning of each sentence, you can use a variety of sentence patterns, including some complex and compound sentences. Here are some sentence patterns. You learned most of this information previously in this chapter.

1. Start with a prepositional phrase: ***On Wednesday*** *we went to the movies.*

(Notice that you don't need a comma after a prepositional phrase that begins a sentence unless it is long or you use two prepositional phrases in a row, for example, "***On Wednesday after lunch***, *we went to the movies.*")

2. Start with an adverb clause: ***When the movie was over***, *we had dinner.*

3. Start with an infinitive phrase: ***To get into the popular movie***, *we had to leave the house early.*

4. Use an adjective clause in your sentence: *The movie*, ***which opened yesterday***, *was crowded.*

5. Use an appositive: *My favorite movie*, ***Star Wars***, *was very popular when it came out.*

6. Begin with a participial phrase: ***Driving home***, *we talked about how great the movie was.*

7. Begin with a **gerund**: (*Gerund* is a new term. A gerund is a verb with an *-ing* ending that is used as a noun, for example, as the subject of a sentence): ***Going*** *to movies is my favorite hobby.*

Helpful Hint! How dull it would be to write the sentences above as simple sentences starting with subjects each time! Take a look . . .

> We went to the movies on Wednesday. We had dinner when the movie was over. We had to leave the house early to get into the popular movie. The movie was crowded. It opened yesterday. The movie was *Star Wars*. It was very popular when it first came out. We talked about how great the movie was when we were driving home. I really like going to the movies.

I have spent most of the day putting in a comma
and the rest of the day taking it out.

—Oscar Wilde, paraphrased

Chapter 3

Punctuation

Punctuation marks are those symbols in writing that let you know where sentences end, when to pause, or which sentences are questions or exclamations. Without punctuation marks it would be nearly impossible to read a paragraph or a page of a book. Common punctuation marks include periods, commas, question marks, quotation marks, exclamation points, semicolons, colons, hyphens, and dashes.

3.1 Periods and Other Ending Punctuation

By ending punctuation, we mean the marks that come at the end of a sentence. Every sentence needs some punctuation at the end. Most sentences end with a period.

Statements, or **declarative sentences,** have a period at the end. Most sentences are declarative.

He went to the party with me.

Imperative sentences, or commands, also have a period at the end.

Take the book to school.

Interrogative sentences, or questions, have a question mark at the end.

Did you go to the party last night?

Exclamatory sentences (sentences that express excitement) have an exclamation point at the end.

There's a fire in the kitchen!

Interjections are also often followed by an exclamation point. In the following example, the sentence could also end with an exclamation point rather than a question mark if it was said in an exclamatory way. However, don't overdo exclamation points, and never use two in a row.

Wow! Did you see that car?

If you have a quote, the period always goes **inside** the quotation marks in American English. (It is the opposite in British English.)

He said, "I always shop on Wednesdays."

The other main use of periods is in abbreviations. Refer to Chapter 8.2.

Helpful Hint! Question marks and exclamation points go inside the quotes if they are part of the quote, and outside if they are not part of the quote.

"Do you have a pencil?" she asked. (The quoted sentence is a question.)

Did you say, "I have no pencil"? (The whole sentence is a question, not the quoted part.)

More about this in Chapter 3.8.

3.2 Commas (,)

Commas have about 700 rules! Well, maybe not 700, but it sure seems that way sometimes. The most important rule is to never use a comma without a reason. Here is a listing of the most common rules with examples for each.

1. Series: Commas are used after each item in a series of three or more items, whether the series is words, phrases, or clauses. The final comma (before *and* or *or*) is optional and is called the Oxford comma.

    I brought shoes, socks, and a jacket. (or *shoes, socks and a jacket*)

    She went to the park, for a drive, and to the grocery store.

2. Compound sentences: Use a comma before the conjunction in a compound sentence unless the two parts are very short.

    She brought her brother home, and she made him dinner.

    I am hungry and I am thirsty. (short; comma not necessary)

Note: Both sides of the conjunction need to be complete sentences; otherwise, the sentence is *not* compound, and you don't use a comma.

She brought her brother home and *made him dinner.* (*Made him dinner* is not a sentence.)

---

3. After introductory clauses: If a sentence starts with a dependent clause, use a comma. Usually there is no comma if the clause comes at the end of the sentence.

    If I get an A on the test, *I will get an A in the course.*

    Because he is a good dog, *I gave him a treat.*

    I gave him a treat **because he is a good dog.**

4. After introductory phrases, words, and expressions unless the phrase is followed by a verb.

    Stretching out on the sofa, *my cat fell asleep.*

    (But . . . **Stretching out on the sofa** *is relaxing.)*

    Finally, *you should proofread your writing.*

    In my opinion, *you are correct.*

> ***On Monday*** *we had a quiz. (not needed after a short preposi-*
> *tional phrase)*
>
> ***No, Susan,*** *you cannot come with us.*

5. Around words, phrases, and clauses that interrupt a sentence and add additional information.

   > *This is,* ***in my opinion,*** *a perfect day!*
   >
   > *My mother,* ***Joanna,*** *is an artist.*
   >
   > *My cat,* ***lying on my bed,*** *is probably asleep.*
   >
   > *Dune,* ***which I read last week,*** *is a famous book.*
   >
   > *I think,* ***however,*** *that you are telling the truth.*

Note: If the phrase or clause is necessary for the meaning of the sentence, use no commas.

> *My brother* ***John*** *is the tallest of us four.* (tells which brother)
>
> *The book* ***that I just read*** *is called* Dune. (tells which book)

---

6. Between two adjectives. Use a comma between two adjectives in a row that describe the same noun if putting *and* between them makes sense.

   > *It is a cold, rainy day.* (*Cold and rainy* makes sense.)
   >
   > *She wore a bright blue dress.* (*Bright* describes *blue,* not *dress.*)
   >
   > *I am giving away my old green coat.* (*Old and green* doesn't make sense.)

7. Before afterthoughts at the end of a sentence (but not the word *too*).

   > *You have finished your essay,* ***haven't you?***
   >
   > *Could you clean up the kitchen,* ***please?***
   >
   > *I want to go* ***too.***

8. In direct address, which is when you call someone by name.

   > ***Jim,*** *could you please come over here.*
   >
   > *Could you please come over here,* ***Jim?***

*I hope, **Jim,** you will help me clean up.*

9. When writing dates that consist of month, day, and year.

   *It is **March 5, 2015.***

   *I need the **March 5, 2015,** issue of the magazine.*

   *It is **March 2015.***

   *I need the **March 2015** issue of the magazine.*

10. In numbers 1,000 and larger and to separate two numbers in a row:

    In 2015, 350 people graduated from this school.

11. Use a comma before the word *or* in a sentence when it represents a definition rather than a choice.

    *He is the drum major, **or** the person who leads the band.*

    *Would you like to be the drum major **or** the lead clarinet?*

12. Around any words that interrupt the flow of the sentence.

    *I bought that cake, **unhealthy as it might be,** to celebrate.*

13. Around *too* in the middle of a sentence when it means *also*. Around *etc., i.e.,* and *e.g.,* when they are in the middle of a sentence.

    *I, **too,** would like to have some pizza.*

    *This is **too** salty for my taste.*

    *We ate chips, nachos, pretzels, **etc.,** at the game.*

    *I take two foreign languages, **i.e.,** French and Spanish.*

    *I love to play sports, **e.g.,** football, hockey, and many more.*

14. To set off academic degrees and titles.

    *Paul Marks, **Ph.D.,** is teaching at my college.*

    *Paul Marks, **Jr.** is teaching at my college.* (No comma is needed after *Jr.* or *Sr.*)

15. In addresses, both on envelopes and in text.

    I live at 35 Main Street, Lexington, MA 02345.

John Stone
35 Main Street
Lexington, MA 02345

16. In contrasting expressions.

    She is small, but strong.

    Here today, gone tomorrow

    I like pizza, but not with anchovies.

17. In company names if they use a comma. In general, spell and punctuate a company name exactly as the company does.

    Marcus Green, Inc.

    ABC Paper Inc.

18. In sentences with unusual word order.

    When he will get here, I don't know.

19. Sometimes you can, optionally, use a comma for emphasis.

    I agree, completely, that you should have come in first.

20. To avoid confusion when a word is left out of a sentence.

    I agree, we don't know all the answers. (The comma replaces *that*, which is left out.)

21. In greetings and closing of letters.

    Dear Janet, (use a colon in business letters: *Dear Dr. Li:)*

    Sincerely yours,

22. To clear up confusion in any sentence.

    As we ate, ants crawled on the blanket.

    The two dresses are blue and white, and red and pink.

Helpful Hint! Do not put a comma between the subject and the verb of a sentence.

The girls, went to the mall yesterday. Incorrect.

The girls went to the mall yesterday. Correct.

3.3 Semicolons (;)

Semicolons are not complicated. And unlike commas, semicolons have only three uses.

1. Use a semicolon in a **compound sentence** (two sentences joined together with the conjunctions *and, or, nor, yet, so, but, for*) when you don't use the conjunction. To use a semicolon, two sentences should be somewhat closely related.

   I ordered the steak; my friend ordered the salmon.

   You can also write this sentence other ways:

   I ordered the steak, and my friend ordered the salmon.

   I ordered the steak. My friend ordered the salmon.

   Do not use both the conjunction and the semicolon in this situation. Use **either** the conjunction or the semicolon.

   Note: Do not begin the second part of the sentence (after the semicolon) with a capital letter.

   ---

2. Use a semicolon in a compound sentence where a conjunction **is** used, if there is a series in one or both parts of the sentence.

   I saw Jenny, Joe, Mark, and Sam; but I didn't see Jim. (This use of the semicolon simply makes things clearer and easier to read— and **clarity** is the purpose of punctuation.)

3. Try to figure out this sentence:

   Mr. Garcia, my Spanish teacher, my math teacher, Mrs. White, a parent, and Mr. Bloom are chaperoning the dance.

   Can you tell how many people we are talking about? How about now?

   Mr. Garcia, my Spanish teacher; my math teacher; Mrs. White, a parent; and Mr. Bloom are chaperoning the dance.

   Four people are chaperoning. It is clear in the second sentence, but not in the first one.

This third rule of the semicolon is to use it in a series if one or more of the items in the series already need commas. Follow **every** item (except the last, of course) with a semicolon even if some of the items don't have commas in them. For example, *my math teacher* is standing by itself, but still has semicolons around it for consistency. Each separate item has a semicolon after it.

3.4 Colons (:)

The most common use of the colon is to introduce a list.

1. Use a colon to introduce a list in a sentence. Many times the words *follow* or *following* are used in the introduction before the colon, but not necessarily. Here are some examples:

   *Please bring the **following** items: a coat, shoes, a hat, and an umbrella.*

   These are some of the items to bring: a coat, shoes, a hat, and an umbrella.

Helpful Hint! **Do not** use a colon if the sentence reads fine as a sentence. In the examples above, if you took the colon out, the words would not read correctly as a sentence. However, look at this sentence:

   Please bring a coat, shoes, a hat, and an umbrella.

You would **not** put a colon after *bring* here because that would cut the sentence up. Do not put a colon between a verb and the list items.

---

2. Colons are also used to introduce a vertical list. Here is an example:

   Please bring the following items:
   • *a coat*
   • *shoes*
   • *a hat*
   • *an umbrella*

Even in a vertical list, you don't put a colon after a verb when the list items complete the sentence.

> *Please bring*
> • *a coat*
> • *shoes*
> • *a hat*
> • *an umbrella*

3. Colons can also be used to separate two sentences if the second sentence follows from the first or is a result of the first. This is not a very common usage and can usually be avoided by simply using two sentences, using a semicolon, or rewriting.

> *There is a meeting on Friday: layoffs and new projects will be discussed at that time.*

Whether you use a semicolon or a colon, do not capitalize the second part of the sentence.

4. The other uses for a colon are, of course, in time (*9:50 a.m.*) and after the salutation (greeting) of a business letter (*Dear Sirs:*).

3.5. Parentheses ( ), Brackets [ ], and Braces { }

Parentheses are used to enclose information that isn't of major importance. You can use parentheses around a single word, a phrase, or a complete sentence. You can put the parentheses within the sentence, or, if the material in parentheses is a complete sentence, you can put it on its own. Here are some examples. Notice the punctuation because it can be confusing if the material in parentheses is a sentence.

1. *Joe Moon (1915–1970) was a great artist in my town.*

2. *Joe Moon (my uncle) was a wonderful artist.*

3. *Joe Moon was a wonderful artist (he was also my uncle).*

4. *Joe Moon was a wonderful artist. (He was my uncle and taught me how to paint.)*

In Example 3, the enclosed material is a complete sentence, but it doesn't require either a capital at the beginning or a period at the end because it is included in the sentence. The period is outside the parentheses and belongs to the entire sentence. In Example 4 the parenthetical information is its own sentence and is placed outside the other sentence. The original sentence has its own period. Therefore, the sentence in parentheses would have a capital letter to begin it and a period to end it.

Brackets are not very common. They are used to add an explanation to quoted material. In this case, always use brackets instead of parentheses.

> *"I love this [dress], and it was designed especially for this occasion."*

In the example, the word *dress* was not in the quote: the quote may have been taken from a longer discussion. We may not have heard or read the rest of the discussion, so *dress* is needed in order for the reader to understand the quote.

Brackets are also used to further explain information that is already in parentheses. If you need parentheses inside of parentheses, you use brackets.

> *Turn to page 65 (the bottom of the page [Review B]), and read the instructions.*

If possible, it is best to rewrite the sentence to avoid using the brackets:

> *Turn to page 65 and refer to Review B at the bottom of the page.*

Braces: Don't even worry about it! Braces are generally used for math and other technical information (and to straighten teeth).

3.6 Hyphens (-) and Dashes (– and —)

Hyphen - (shortest)

En dash – (medium)

Em dash — (longest)

Okay, so what's the difference among these three?

Hyphen

A hyphen is used in some compound words (two words that are put together as one word); it is also used when you split a word at the end of a line.

1. Some compound words are hyphenated. There is no general rule as to when you hyphenate a word. Generally, when a word is new, it is two separate words; as the word becomes more common, it becomes hyphenated. When it becomes really common, it is often written as one word.

   Web site, web-site, and website. The best thing to do is look in the dictionary; otherwise, take your best guess.

Helpful Hints!

1. A compound word that comes right before a noun it is describing is generally hyphenated. When it comes after the noun, it is not generally hyphenated:

   *He is a **well-known painter**. The painter is very **well known**.*

   *He is a **ten-year-old boy**. The boy is a **ten year old**.*

2. If you are unsure about whether to hyphenate a word, and you cannot find it in the dictionary (or if dictionaries disagree), pick one way to write it, and be consistent within one piece of writing.

---

2. A hyphen is used to split a word when you don't have room to write the whole word on the line. With computers, this problem is somewhat outdated. However, if you do have to split a word at the end of a line, you must split it between syllables. This means you cannot ever split a one-syllable word. You can look up where the syllables split in the dictionary. There is usually a vowel in each syllable. If the word has a double consonant, such as *happen*, the word is split between the double consonant (*hap pen*).

En Dash

The **en dash** is the shorter of the two dashes. Some people just hit the hyphen twice. Sometimes the computer puts them together for you. You can also press the Control key and the hyphen on the number pad in Word/Windows, or press the Command key and the hyphen on the number pad in Word/Mac to get an en dash. The main use of the en dash is to indicate a range of numbers or dates, for example, *pages 64–67.* The en dash is also used for the minus sign. Many people use the en dash where the em dash should be. If you are using a copyeditor, he or she may change it to an em dash.

Em Dash

The em dash is the long one that you use to indicate a break in your sentence. On my Mac, I press shift/option/hyphen to make the long dash. You can sometimes use parentheses instead of a dash (and sometimes maybe even commas), but generally an em dash is used to indicate a bigger break in your thoughts. Be careful about where you put the dash: the sentence should still make sense if you take the text between the dashes out. Dashes are often overused. Use them only when indicating an abrupt change in thought in your sentences.

> *Our vacation—if we can afford to take one this year—will be a trip to Europe.*

Helpful Hint! There are usually no spaces before or after hyphens or dashes.

3.7 Italics

While not a punctuation mark, italics seem to fit here. *Italics* are those slanted words you sometimes see in books or magazines. You cannot write italics by hand; use italics for printed material only. To italicize something when you are writing by hand, you underline it instead. There is often confusion about which things are in quotes and which things are in italics.

1. Italicize titles of big things: book titles, titles of plays, titles of operas, titles of television series, titles of CDs, and other complete works. Parts of these works—shorter things—are quoted: chapter titles, short story titles, titles of television series' episodes, and titles of songs are in quotes.

2. Use italics when you are referring to a letter, a number, or a word as itself.

   My name begins with an *A*.

   The word *queue* is difficult for me to spell.

   My lucky numbers are 2 and *8*.

3. Sometimes italics are used for emphasis. It is better to use italics than either bold or all caps for emphasis.

3.8 Quotation ("") and Single (') Quotation Marks

Quotation marks have two main uses: to enclose direct quotations (the exact words someone says) and to enclose titles of short works. (Note that I use the words *quotes* and *quotation marks* interchangeably. They are the same thing.)

1. Enclosing titles: In Chapter 3.7 we discussed putting titles of books, plays, television series, CDs, operas, and other long works in *italics* (or underlining them in handwritten text).

   For short works, such as short stories, chapter titles, a single episode of a TV series, or a song, use quotation marks.

2. Direct quotes: You must use quotation marks around direct quotes, the exact words that someone says.

   John said, "I am hungry." (Direct quote)

   John said that he was hungry. (Not a direct quote, so no quotation marks)

Here are some rules to follow when quoting:

- The direct quote starts with a capital letter.

  He said, "We want our pie."

- In a split quotation, the second part does **not** begin with a capital letter.

  "I want my pie," he said, "and the rest of my lunch!"

- Notice that commas, not periods, are used to set off quoted portions from the rest of the sentence.

  "I want my pie," he said. Correct

  "I want my pie." he said. Incorrect

- In American English, periods and commas are *always* placed inside quotation marks. Question marks and exclamation points can go either inside or outside quotation marks. If they are part of the quote, they are placed inside the quote. If they are part of the entire sentence, they are placed outside the quotes. Here are some examples of punctuation with quotes:

  "I want my pie," he said.

  He said, "I want my pie."

  Did he say, "I want my pie"? (Notice there is no period after *pie.* Only one piece of punctuation is used, the question mark. The question mark refers to the whole sentence.)

  He asked, "Where is my pie?" (Here, the question mark is part of the quote, so it is placed inside the quotation marks.)

  "I lost my pie!" he exclaimed.

  It scared me when he said, "I want my pie"! (The whole sentence is an exclamation, not the quote.)

  Did he ask, "Where is my pie?" (Here, **both** the quote and the whole sentence are questions. Use one question mark, and put it inside the quotation marks.)

Single Quotes

Use single quotes only when you need to put quotes inside of quotes.

She said, "I read the short story 'Mother and Me' for my essay." (The short story title needs quotes around it.)

She said, "I read the short story 'Mother and Me.'" (There is a single quote for the story and double quotes for the quote, so there are three quotes at the end of the sentence. The ending quotation marks have no spaces between them.)

3.9 Ellipses (. . .)

An ellipsis is used to take the place of omitted words in a quote or to indicate trailing off at the end of a sentence. It is made with three periods with a space between each, as well as a space before and after. If you are leaving words out of a quote, make sure the meaning is still apparent. If there is a sentence before the ellipsis, there would be a period and then the three ellipsis periods. If the ellipsis ends the sentence, there is still ending punctuation unless you are using the ellipsis to indicate trailing off.

He said, "I'm going . . . and you cannot stop me." (words are left out)

He said, "I'm going. . . . you won't stop me." (ellipsis begins new sentence)

She said, "I am going right now . . . !" (words left out at end of sentence)

She thought about her children and her friends and . . . (trailing off)

(P.S. Yes, I find them confusing too!)

3.10 Apostrophes (')

Apostrophes are often misused. They have two main uses: 1. to indicate missing letters in a contraction and 2. to indicate possession.

1. Contractions are words that are put together to make a shorter word: *I'm* instead of *I am*, *it's* instead of *it is*, *couldn't* instead of *could not*. The apostrophe is put where the missing letter(s) would be.

2. Apostrophes are used to indicate possession:

*My **brother's** boat is in this marina.* (singular noun possessive)

*My **brothers'** houses are on this street.* (plural noun possessive)

***Thomas's** house is on this street.* (singular ending in *s* possessive)

This is ***yours/its/hers/his/ours/theirs***: There is no apostrophe in possessive pronouns.

3. Okay. There is *no* apostrophe in most plurals. The plural of *brother* is *brothers*, not *brother's*! The only time you use an apostrophe in a plural is for clarity: There are too many *a*'s in this word. However, you do not need an apostrophe in these plurals: The *1900s*. The *PTAs* (abbreviation with all caps).

I always put the apostrophe in "ain't"
to make certain I'm using proper improper English.
—*Author unknown*

Chapter 4

Capitalization

Yikes! There are so many rules for capitalization! The basic rule is to capitalize the names of proper nouns (specific people, places, and things).

Don't capitalize *boy*, but capitalize ***Robert***.

Don't capitalize *school*, but capitalize ***Blair High School***.

Don't capitalize *summer*, but capitalize ***Fourth of July***.

Places and things that contain more than one word, such as Fourth of July, follow the same capitalization rules as titles (see Chapter 8.1).

In a nutshell, here are the rules for capitalization:

1. Capitalize the first word of every sentence. You do not need to capitalize the word after a colon even if it begins a complete sentence.

2. Capitalize the first word only of the greeting and closing of a letter:

    Dear Sirs, Yours truly, Sincerely yours, To whom it may concern
    (Sirs is a title, so it is capitalized)

3. Capitalize the pronoun *I*.

4. Capitalize people's and animals' names:

    Julie, Fido, Spot, Mr. Jones

5. Capitalize cities, states, countries, continents, oceans, islands, streets, mountains, forests, and regions of the country:

   San Francisco, Texas, United States, North America, Atlantic Ocean, Mississippi River, Main Street, the Alps, Yosemite National Park, New England, and the *Middle East*

Helpful Hint! Do not capitalize north, south, east, and west when they indicate direction. **Do** capitalize them if they are used to name a region.

She is from the South.

I need to travel south on this highway.

---

6. Capitalize the names of clubs, teams, and government bodies:

   Parent-Teacher Organization, Boston Celtics, Middletown City Council

7. Capitalize holidays, events, and historical periods:

   Fourth of July, Labor Day, Oklahoma State Fair, Revolutionary War

8. Capitalize the names of nationalities, races, and peoples:

   French, African American, Navajo

9. Capitalize businesses and brand names the same way they capitalize them—or not: (Note that some businesses may not capitalize their names.)

   Central Bank, Tasty Soup, Sally's Cleaning, bigwords101.

10. Capitalize the names of ships, trains, spacecraft, and aircraft:

    Mayflower, Apollo 10

11. Capitalize the names of buildings and other structures:

    Bristol Building, Golden Gate Bridge, Towne Theater

12. Capitalize the names of awards, monuments, and memorials:

    Academy Award, Lincoln Memorial, Newbury Medal, Nobel Peace Prize

13. Capitalize religions, holy books, and some deities:

    Christianity, Judaism, Hinduism, Protestant, the Bible, God, the god Neptune. (Note that the word *god* is not capitalized when it refers to a mythological god.)

14. Capitalize planets, stars, constellations, and other heavenly bodies:

    Mars, Orion's Belt, the Milky Way.

    Sun and *moon* are not capitalized. *Earth* is capitalized when spoken about with other planets that are capitalized; otherwise, it usually is not:

    Jupiter and Saturn are farther from the sun than Earth is.

    The earth is not flat.

15. Capitalize a person's title if it comes before the name:

    Mr. Jones, Dr. Medina, Mayor Ling

    I am seeing the doctor today.

    Are you voting for mayor?

16. Capitalize a word that shows a family relationship if it comes before the name or is used in place of the name:

    Aunt Mary, but *my aunt; Mom,* but *my mom*

17. Capitalize most words in titles. Do not capitalize conjunctions, small prepositions, and articles. See Chapter 8.1.

> You know you're a language nerd
> when you have a strong opinion about serial commas.
>
> —*Author unknown*

Chapter 5

Things to Avoid

This chapter contains some of the things you just shouldn't do when you write, particularly when you write in a school or business setting. Academic and business writing is formal, and you don't want to write the way you might text or talk to friends.

5.1 Dead Words

Eliminate "dead" words from your writing and, if necessary, use a thesaurus to find a better word. Here are some dead words to avoid:

- *A lot*—too informal. However, if you must occasionally use it, it is two separate words (not *alot*).
- *Good* and *bad*—too common. Come on—you can do better! Same goes for *great*.
- *Stuff, things, bunch*—Be specific! Use *bunch* only when you are talking about bananas.

- *Nice, fun,* and other boring adjectives (by the way, *funner* and *funnest* are not words!).
- *Really, very,* and other boring adverbs. Instead of these two words, try *unusually, fully, extensively, certainly, extremely, incredibly, exceptionally, remarkably, particularly,* or *exceedingly.*
- *Cool, awesome,* and all slang and overused words.
- *Gonna, shoulda, woulda, coulda*—these are not words at all!
- *Nite, lite,* and other incorrect shorthand spellings.
- *Have got*—just *have* is enough! Example: *I have a dog.* Not *I have got a dog.*

5.2 Anywheres, Anyways

Anywheres, nowheres, somewheres, and *anyways* are not words. There is no *s* at the end of these words. The same is also true for *ways* if you are talking about distance: *I have a long way to go,* **not** *I have a long ways to go.*

5.3 Wasted Words

1. *The fact that* is a wasted phrase. You don't need those words at all.

   Use: *You should know that I am moving away.*

   Don't use: *You should know the fact that I am moving away.*

   Use: *I am the chairperson.*

   Don't use: *The fact that I am the chairperson is important.*

2. Hopefully, everyone knows by now that you don't put the pronoun after the noun.

   Wrong: *John <u>he</u> went to the store.*

   Right: *John went to the store.* **OR**

       He went to the store.

3. *Kind of* and *sort of* are wasted words:

   Don't use: *This lettuce is kind of wilted.*

   Use: *This lettuce is wilted.* **OR** *This lettuce is slightly wilted.*

Don't use: *I am sort of tired.*

Use: *I am tired.* **OR** *I am a little tired.*

5.4 A Comma to Separate Sentences

You have already read about this in Chapter 2.9. **Never** separate two complete sentences with a comma—unless you are also using a conjunction. You need a period or a semicolon to separate two sentences (without using a conjunction). Otherwise, you have a run-on, otherwise known as a **comma splice**.

Incorrect: *I went to the movies, my brother could not go with me.*

Correct: *I went to the movies. My brother could not go with me.* **OR**

I went to the movies; my brother could not go with me. **OR**

I went to the movies, but my brother could not go with me.

5.5 *Could Of/Should Of/Would Of*

Do not use *could of, should of,* or *would of.* Of course, it goes without saying that we don't use *coulda, shoulda,* or *woulda* (or *gonna*)!

The correct way to write these phrases is as follows:

Could have

Should have

Would have

Always use *have* with these words, not *of.*

5.6 *Firstly, Secondly, Thirdly, Lastly*

These words are generally used as transitions. Do not use these words. Use *first, second, third, last,* and *finally* instead.

5.7 Double Negatives

Most of us know not to use the usual double negatives, but there are some double negatives that are not as obvious. A double negative is using two negative words in a row (which actually turns into a positive) and is not standard. Here are some double negatives:

- *I don't have no money*—should be *I don't have any money.*
- *I haven't got no money*—should be *I don't have any money.*
- *I haven't barely any money*—should be *I have barely any money.* (*Barely* is a negative.)
- *I haven't hardly begun*—should be *I have hardly begun.* (*Hardly* is a negative.)
- *I could care less*—This common saying is not correct, and actually *should* be a double negative! It should be *I couldn't care less.* Think about the meaning: if you *could* care less, then you do care some—which is probably not what you mean to say.

5.8 *Irregardless*

Many of us use the word *irregardless*. And you will find it in the dictionary. However, it is much better to use the preferred word (which means the same thing): *regardless.*

Regardless of the consequences, I am going to sail around the world in my small boat.

5.9 Unclear Pronouns and Antecedents

First of all, what is an **antecedent**? In Chapter 1.2, we talked about pronouns. Pronouns substitute for a noun or other pronoun in a sentence. The **antecedent** is the noun (or pronoun) that the pronoun is standing in for.

Sue took *her* book back to the library. The noun *Sue* is the antecedent of the pronoun *her.* You wouldn't want to say, *Sue brought Sue's book back to the library.* Pronouns really come in handy, so you don't need to keep repeating the noun.

However, when you use a pronoun, be sure that the reader can tell what the pronoun refers to; otherwise, you have an unclear antecedent. Common pronouns with unclear antecedents tend to involve the pronouns *this* and *which*.

> *I had two papers to write during the weekend, and I also had a math test to study for. **This** made things difficult.*

It isn't really clear what the pronoun *this* refers to. Does it refer to the papers? The test? We don't know. The pronouns *this* and *which* should always refer to one noun or pronoun. They should not be used to represent a whole idea.

Unclear: *I had a really busy weekend. **This** made it difficult to study.*

What made it difficult to study?

Better: *I couldn't study much because I had a busy weekend.*

OR *My busy weekend made it difficult to study.*

(There are also other ways to write this idea.)

Unclear: *He is a really good friend, **which** is nice for me.*

What is nice for you?

Better: *I am glad that he is a really good friend to me.*

Also be careful with the pronoun *it*.

Unclear: *This past weekend I went camping and hiking. **It** was really nice.*

What was really nice?

Better: *This past weekend I went camping and hiking. These activities were really fun.*

5.10 *Got* Instead of *Have*

Do not use *got* when you really mean *have*.

> *I don't got any books* should be *I don't have any books.*

Have you got any money? should be *Do you have any money? (Have* means *"to own.")*

I got a new car for my birthday is correct. (*Got* means *"received"* or *"obtained."*)

5.11 Flat Adverbs

We discussed adverbs in Chapter 1.5. Adverbs "describe" verbs (or sometimes adjectives or other adverbs). And to review, adjectives describe nouns (or pronouns). Here are some examples of adverbs:

* *He talks quietly.* (*Quietly* is an adverb that tells how he talks.)
* *We will leave soon.* (*Soon* is an adverb that tells when we will leave.)
* *He talks extremely quietly.* (*Extremely* is an adverb describing another adverb—*quietly*—that tells to what extent.)
* *She is really pretty.* (*Really* is an adverb describing the adjective *pretty*, telling to what extent.)

You have probably noticed that most adverbs end in *-ly*. However, there are also other words that end in *-ly*, mainly adjectives like *lovely, lonely,* and *daily.*

So, not all adverbs end in *-ly*, and not all words that end in *-ly* are adverbs.

Most of the adverbs that end in *-ly* are created from the adjective, which has no *-ly*:

* *quiet* is an adjective (quiet house), but *quietly* is an adverb (talk quietly).
* *soft* is an adjective (soft blanket), but *softly* is an adverb (speak softly).

You get the idea.

A **flat adverb** is an adverb without an *-ly* at the end.

Soon, now, then, later, too, very . . . adverbs with no *-ly*. Easy.

But what about these sentences?

*Drive **slow** because the roads are slippery.* Drive *slow*. Well, you could have said *drive slowly*, which is definitely preferred.

*You went **fast** through those curvy roads. You went fast.* There is no *fastly. Fast* is both an adjective (*fast car*) and an adverb (*drive fast*). So using this flat adverb is fine.

*You need to come **clean** about what happened. Come clean.* Here is a case where the *-ly* form is different from the flat form. *The wound healed cleanly is fine,* but you wouldn't say *come cleanly*. So either form is fine, depending on what you mean.

*He hit the ball **hard**. Hit hard* makes sense. But if you say *hardly hit,* well, that is the opposite. So, in this case the flat adverb and the *-ly* form are opposites!

Rule of thumb: Flat adverbs used to be more common. Now, if there is an *-ly* version of the adverb that says what you mean, use it.

5.12 Redundancy: Repeating Yourself

Be careful when you write, and also when you speak, not to use words and phrases that are redundant, or to say the same thing twice. It is easier to catch these redundancies in writing than in speaking because in speaking you cannot go back and edit!

Here are some examples of redundancies:

1. *We cut the cost by 30 percent less.* If we cut the cost, of course it was less! You don't need the word *less* here. *We cut the cost by 30 percent* is enough.

2. *It is completely unique.* Something is either unique or it isn't. You don't need the word *completely. It is unique.*

3. *It is my personal opinion.* If it is your opinion, it is personal, so you don't need the word *personal* there. *It is my opinion.*

4. *She is very small in size. Small* generally refers to size, so you don't need to say *size. She is very small.*

5. *Count each and every one of them. Each* and *every* are the same. You need only one of the words. *Count every one of them.*

6. *I have not finished the project as yet. Yet* is sufficient without *as. I have not finished the project yet.*

These are many more redundant words and phrases, so choose your words carefully. Just something else to think about.

A preposition is a terrible thing to end a sentence with.
—*Winston S. Churchill*

Chapter 6

Confusing Things

This chapter discusses words and phrases that are often confused.

6.1 *Affect/Effect*

These two are tough! Each can be either a noun or a verb. Most of the time, *affect* is a verb and *effect* is a noun. Here is the correct usage:

*How does the hot weather **affect** you?*

*What **effect** does the hot weather have on you?*

Occasionally, the words are used differently. *Effect* can be used as a verb, and *affect* can be used as a noun. Here are examples:

*He had a rather quiet **affect.*** Means "a way of being." Note that the word is pronounced differently as a noun. The first syllable is stressed, and the *a* is short like in the word *absent* (a' fekt).

*The new president will try to **effect** some changes in the country.*

6.2 *Already/All Ready*

Already is an adverb. It refers to time. Here are the correct usages:

*Did you get home **already**?*

*Are you **all ready** to go to the party?*

6.3 *Alright/All Right*

This one is easy! *Alright* is slang, so don't use it at all. The correct words are always *all right*, no matter how the phrase is used.

*I asked the man if he was **all right** after the accident.*

*Is it **all right** if I go with you?*

6.4 *Among/Between*

These two words are both prepositions. Use *between* when you are talking about **two** things. Use *among* when there are **more than two**. Here is the correct usage:

*Divide the pie **between** the two of you.*

*Divide the pie **among** the three of us.*

6.5 *Bad/Badly*

Bad is an adjective, and *badly* is an adverb. Use *badly* if you are modifying an action verb. Use *bad* to modify a noun or after a linking verb (as a **predicate adjective**; refer to Chapter 2.4). Here is the correct usage:

*I feel **bad** about the accident.* (*Feel* is a linking verb, linking *I* and *bad*. *Bad* is an adjective describing the pronoun *I*.)

*She performed **badly** on the test.* (*Badly* is an adverb describing the action verb *performed*. Performed how? *Badly*.)

6.6 *By Accident/On Accident*

Many people, especially younger folks, are saying *on accident*—like *on purpose*. However, the correct phrase is *by accident*.

*The baby spilled the milk **by accident**.*

*The baby threw the food **on purpose**.*

6.7 *Data*

Data is actually a plural word. The singular form is *datum*, but *datum* is rarely used. *Data* means information, and the plural use is generally fine, even with a singular verb.

*This **data is** quite interesting.* (You usually wouldn't say *the data are interesting* even though *are* is the plural verb.)

6.8 *Further/Farther*

These two words can be confusing! *Farther* means *"a greater distance."* *Further* means *"additional."* Here is the correct usage:

*My house is **farther** away from school than yours is.*

*I cannot run **farther** than ten miles.*

*We can discuss this **further** later.*

*My essay needs **further** work.*

6.9 *Good/Well*

Refer back to Chapter 6.5. *Good* and *well* are similar to *bad* and *badly*. *Good* is an adjective, and *well* is an adverb. Therefore, use *well* if you are modifying an action verb. Use *good* to modify a noun or after a linking verb (as a predicate adjective. Refer back to Chapter 2.4). Here is the correct usage:

> *I feel **good** about my performance.* (*Feel* is a linking verb. *Good* describes *I*.)

> *She did **well** on the test because she studied.* (*Well* is an adverb describing the action verb *did*. She did *how*?)

There is, however, another use for *well*. If someone asks you how you are, you can say, "*I am good*," which is grammatically correct (adjective after the linking verb *am*). However, you can also say, "*I am well*," because *well* is acceptable when used as a state of health. You can always say, "*I am fine*," and avoid the issue!

6.10 *I/Me* and *Who/Whom*

This can be a tough one!

Here is the story . . .

There are these "things" called **cases** in the English language—and other languages too. Latin has five; English has only three, and we are going to concern ourselves with only two of them: **subjective case** and **objective case**. In English, only pronouns have case issues that concern us. When the pronoun is the subject of the sentence (or a predicate nominative, a pronoun that follows a linking verb like *to be*), you use the subjective case. When the pronoun is a direct object, an indirect object, or the object of a preposition, you use the objective case. Refer to Chapter 2.1, 2.2, 2.3, and 2.4 for information about subjects, predicate nominatives, and objects.

Subjective Case	Objective Case
I	me
we	us
he	him
she	her
they	them
who	whom

I went to the store. (*I* is the subject of the sentence.)

He and I went to the store. (Both pronouns are the subjects of the sentence.)

*I gave **her** the money.* (*I* is the subject, and *her* is the indirect object.)

*I gave Sue and **her** the money.* (*Sue* and *her* are both indirect objects.)

*He gave **him** and **me** the money.* (*Him* and *me* are both indirect objects.)

*He gave the money to **him** and **me**.* (*Him* and *me* are both objects of the preposition *to*.)

***Who** is that man over there?* (*Who* is the subject.)

*To **whom** did you give the money?* (*Whom* is the object of the preposition *to*.)

***Whom** did you see?* (Change the question to a statement and you get *You did see whom. Whom* is the direct object. *You* is the subject.)

Helpful Hints!

1. People seem to run into problems when there are two pronouns, or a name and a pronoun, after the verb. For example: *He saw **Mike** and **I** at the movies.* You wouldn't say, "*He saw **I** at the movies*," would you? Therefore, you wouldn't say, "*He saw Mike and **I** at the movies*." The correct sentence is *He saw Mike and **me** at the movies.*

   Take one of the pronouns away, or the name away, and see if the sentence sounds right.

2. Pronouns often come after words like *for, with, to,* and *from.* Since these words are prepositions, the pronouns after them are objects of the preposition and are in objective case. For example: *Please take a picture **of him and her.***

6.11 *Imply/Infer*

To *imply* is to suggest something without coming right out and saying it.

To *infer* is to conclude something from what has been said or suggested.

These two words are similar, but opposite. You can imply something; someone else will listen to you and infer something from what you said. Or, someone may imply something by what they say; you will then infer something from what they said.

*Jane **implied** that she would not be attending the party.*

*I **inferred** from what Jane said that she would not be attending the party.*

6.12 *Its/It's*

It's means "*it is.*" It is a contraction.

Its is a possessive. It does not mean "*it is.*"

Remember that all contractions have apostrophes (*I'm, it's, she'll, don't*).

Possessive pronouns never have apostrophes (*Its, ours, yours, theirs*).

***It's** raining today.* (*It is* raining today.)

*The dog ate **its** food.* (The food belongs to the dog. *Its* is possessive here. It does not mean "*it is.*")

6.13 *Lay/Lie*

In Chapter 1.3 we talked about verbs. You may want to look back there now to refresh your memory about transitive and intransitive verbs. Transitive verbs have a direct object; intransitive verbs do not.

The verb *lay* is transitive. It has a direct object.

The verb *lie* is intransitive. It does not have a direct object.

In other words, you must *lay* something, but you don't *lie* something.

> *I will **lay** my hat on the table.* (Lay what? Hat. *Hat* is the direct object.)

> *She **lies** in the sun.* (Lies what? Nothing. *Lies* has no direct object.)

> *She **is laying** a blanket on the bed.* (Laying what? Blanket.)

> *The dog **is lying** on its back.* (Lying what? **Lying** has no direct object.)

Part of the problem with these two verbs concerns the forms for the different tenses, which are quite confusing. Here are examples of the correct usage for each verb.

Lie	Lay
I **lie** down.	I **lay** my coat on the chair.
Yesterday, I **lay** down. (past)	Yesterday, I **laid** my coat on the chair. (past)
I have often **lain** down. (present perfect)	I have often **laid** my coat on the chair. (present perfect)

Part of the confusion is that the past tense of *lie* is *lay*. However, the past tense of *lay* is *laid*. No wonder we are all confused!

6.14 *Less/Fewer*

The difference between *less* and *fewer* can be tricky. *Less* is used with things that cannot be counted and tells "how much." *Fewer* is used with plural words and tells "how many."

> *I use **less** salt when I cook than my mother did.* (**Salt** cannot be counted.)

> *There were **fewer** people at Disneyland today.* (**People** is plural and can be counted.)

6.15 *Like/As If*

Like is a preposition and introduces a phrase. *As* and *as if* are coordinating conjunctions and introduce clauses (see Chapter 2.6).

*She looks **like a model**.* (prepositional phrase)

*She looks **as if** she might be a model.* (Do not say *like she might be a model; she might be a model* is a clause with a subject and a verb.)

Helpful Hint! Don't use *like* if there is a verb in what follows.

6.16 *Only*: Where To Put It

Only is an adverb. Be careful where you put it in a sentence because different placements of the word *only* can change the meaning of a sentence. Check it out:

*She **only** danced in the talent show.* (She danced, but she didn't do anything else.)

*She danced **only** in the talent show.* (She didn't dance anywhere else.)

*She danced in the **only** talent show.* (There was no other talent show.)

***Only** she danced in the talent show.* (No one else danced in the show.)

Here is the usual misplacement of the word *only*:

We only made five dollars should be *We made only five dollars.*

See what I mean?

Note: Be careful with the word *almost* too. Note the difference in meaning here:

We almost made five dollars. (We may have made nothing.)

We made almost five dollars. (We could have made $4.99.)

6.17 *Principal/Principle*

There are two spellings of this word and four different meanings. Three are nouns, and the other can be either a noun or an adjective:

*I had to go to the **principal's** office because I was talking too much in class.* (Head of a school)

*He explained to me the **principles** of behaving in the classroom.* (Rules or ethics)

She has a principal role in the play. (The main one; can be an adjective or a noun)

My mortgage is calculated as both principal and interest. (The money type of principal)

6.18 *Stationary/Stationery*

The *stationary* with the *-ary* means stays in one place. Think of the *a* in station**a**ry and the *a* in pl**a**ce. The *stationery* with the *e* is the one on which you write.

For exercise I ride a stationary bike.

Computers have made paper stationery less common.

6.19 *Than/Then*

Then is an adverb. It tells when: *What did you do then?*

Note: It is important to know that **then** is NOT a conjunction and cannot join two sentences together. You need a conjunction to use with **then**.

*I ate dinner, **then** I went to the movies.* (Incorrect: Run-on sentence)

*I ate dinner, **and then** I went to the movies.* (Correct)

Don't get *than* confused with *then*. *Than* is used in comparisons.

*I am taller **than** he is.*

6.20 *That/Who/Which*

That, who, and *which* are pronouns (see Chapter 1.2); they can be used to begin an adjective clause (see Chapter 2.6). *Who* is used for people, and *which* is used for things.

> *The dress,* **which** *was on sale, is blue and white.*

> *Mr. Frank,* **who** *is my neighbor, is going to France next week.*

That is generally used for things in **essential clauses**; those are the clauses without commas around them because you cannot leave them out.

> *This is the dress* **that** *I wore to the wedding.* (*That I wore to the wedding* is necessary information that identifies which dress. You wouldn't leave it out, you probably would not pause before and after saying it and, therefore, you would not put commas around it.)

Note that *who* is used for people in both nonessential and essential clauses: *He is the boy* **who** *was in the accident.*

6.21 *They're/Their/There*

They're is the contraction that means *they are.*

Their is a possessive pronoun that shows ownership.

There is an adverb that tells where.

> **They're** *going to the movies today.* (*They are* going to the movies today.)

> **Their** *house is for sale.* (The house belongs to them.)

> *The cup is over* **there**. (Tells where.)

6.22 *To/Too/Two*

Two is a number.

To is a preposition.

Too means *also.* It can also mean *very.*

> *I have* **two** *pencils.*

*I am going **to** school now.*

*Are you going **too**? I, **too**, am going. It is **too** far to walk.*

Note: When *too* means *also* (in the last example above), notice that you do <u>not</u> need a comma when *too* is at the end of the sentence. However, if *too* interrupts the sentence, it is set off with commas.

6.23 *Toward/Towards*

Toward and *towards* mean the same thing. You can use either word, but *toward* is preferred in American English. In British English, *towards* is more common.

6.24 *Try and/Try to*

Try and is incorrect. Use *try to* instead.

> ***Try to** eat the vegetables.* (Correct)

> ***Try and** eat the vegetables.* (Incorrect)

6.25 *Who's/Whose*

Who's means *who is*. It is a contraction. *Whose* is possessive.

> ***Who's** coming to dinner? (**Who is** coming to dinner?)*

> ***Whose** book is this? (**Whose** implies ownership. It doesn't mean **who is**.)*

6.26 *Vice Versa*

Vice versa means "*and the other way around.*" Most people know this, but sometimes they say *visa versa*. It is just *vice versa*.

Grammar, which knows how to control even kings.
—Molière

Chapter 7

Important Grammar Issues

This chapter covers some ways to improve your writing and things to watch out for.

7.1 Agreement

By **agreement** we mean that singular subjects go with singular verbs, and a singular pronoun has a singular antecedent. (Remember that the antecedent is the word—noun or pronoun—that the pronoun is standing in for.)

He is a medical student. (*He* is a singular pronoun, and *is* is a singular verb form. They agree.)

Olivia is having a party at her house. (*Olivia* is one female; *her* refers back to *Olivia* and is a singular, female pronoun. They agree.)

Subject/Verb Agreement

How can you tell if a verb is singular? Try using the verb with *he* and *they*. The form of the verb that sounds right with *he* is singular, and the form of the verb that sounds right with *they* is plural.

> **He runs** *three miles each day.* **They run** *three miles each day.*

Runs is the singular verb form, and **run** is the plural verb form. (Notice that this is opposite of nouns, where the plural form has the *s* at the end.)

Pronoun/Verb Agreement

Most problems with pronouns and agreement concern the **indefinite** pronouns, such as *none, everyone, some, neither, either, anyone, someone, few, many, all,* etc. Most of these pronouns are singular; a few of them are plural. Some can be either singular or plural. (See Chapter 1.2 for more information about pronouns.)

Some singular indefinite pronouns: anybody, somebody, everybody, nobody, anything, everything, something, nothing, no one, everyone, someone, anyone, each, either, neither, nothing, one

Some plural indefinite pronouns: both, few, many, several

Pronouns that can be either: all, any, more, most, some, none

Singular pronouns agreeing with singular verbs:

> **Everyone is** *going to the party.*

> **Each** *of us* **is** *planning a vacation* (not **are** planning).

Plural pronouns agreeing with plural verbs:

> **Both are** *fine with me.*

> **Few** *of us* **are** *going.*

Pronouns that can be either:

> **Most** *of the cake* **is** *gone.*

> **Most** *of the people* **are** *going.*

The word in the prepositional phrase following the pronoun determines whether the verb should be singular or plural (*cake* is singular; *people* is plural).

Pronoun/Antecedent Agreement

Once again, the problems are with those indefinite pronouns!

*Everyone is bringing **his or her** friend.* (Use ***his or her*** because it must agree with ***everyone***, which is a singular pronoun—even though it sounds as if it would be plural.)

*Many are bringing **their** friends.* (Use ***their*** because it must agree with ***many***, which is plural.)

Refer back to Chapter 1.2 for a discussion on the singular *"they."* Instead of using the rather awkward *"his or her,"* it is now acceptable to use *they* to agree with a singular antecedent like *everyone.* Do I like it? No. Will I use it? No, not in formal writing. In my opinion, the best solution is to rewrite your sentence to avoid the entire issue: *All the people are bringing friends.*

Agreement with Conjunctions

Rule 1: Two words connected with *and* are always considered plural and take a plural verb and a plural pronoun.

*Every morning **John and James take their** dog for a walk.* (Use *their* and *take* because they are plural and agree with *John and James*, which is also plural.)

Rule 2: Two words connected with *either/or* or *neither/nor* are singular if both of the words are singular.

*Neither **John nor James is bringing his** date to the party.* (*Neither John nor James* is singular, so you use *is*, the singular verb, and *his*, the singular pronoun.)

Rule 3: As if this isn't all confusing enough, when two words are connected with *either/or* or *neither/nor* and one is plural and one is singular, the verb (or pronoun) agrees with the word closer to it.

Neither the boy nor the girls are bringing their *dates.* (Since *girls* is plural and closer to the verb and pronoun than *boy* is, use the plural verb *are bringing* and the plural pronoun *their.*) **BUT**

Neither the girls nor the boy is bringing his *date.* (Since *boy* is singular and closer to the verb and pronoun, use the singular verb *is bringing* and the singular pronoun *his.*)

Collective Noun Agreement with Verb and Pronoun

Remember that a collective noun (see Chapter 1.1) is a singular noun that refers to a group, such as *family*, *band*, *club*, *class*, or *flock*. If the collective noun is referring to the group as a whole, it is considered singular and takes a singular verb. If the collective noun refers to each member of the group separately, it is considered plural and takes a plural verb. This can sometimes be difficult to figure out, and is not generally a big deal if you use the singular rather than the plural verb.

*My **family is taking** a trip this summer.* (Since the whole family is going together, *family* is considered singular, and we use the singular verb *is.*)

*My **family are going** to different places for Thanksgiving this year.* (Since everyone is going to a different place, we are referring to the members of the family separately, and we use the plural verb form *are.*)

*The **band is** marching in the parade.* (They are all marching together.)

*The **band are** tuning their instruments.* (We assume that each member is tuning his or her particular instrument separately.)

7.2 Comparison

Comparison involves adjectives and adverbs.

*I am **tall**.*

*My brother is **taller** than I am.* (The *-er* form is called **comparative** and is used to compare two things or people.)

*My sister is the **tallest** of all of us.* (The *-est* form is called **superlative** and is used to compare more than two things or people.)

Some adjectives do not have *-er* and *-est* forms. For example, there is no such word as *funner* or *funnest*. (Please do not use them!) With these words, you use *more* and *most* in front of them.

*Tennis is **more fun** than golf.*

*Surfing is the **most fun** of all three sports!*

Note: Do not use *more* or *most* with *-er* or *-est*:

Incorrect: *This room is more cleaner than that one.*

Correct: *This room is cleaner than that one.*

Adverbs do not have *-er* and *-est* forms. With adverbs, use *more* and *most*.

*She sang **quietly**.*

*He sang **more quietly** than she did.*

*I sang the **most quietly** of all.*

Helpful Hint! Watch out for "faulty comparison."

She likes pizza more than me.

Does that mean that she likes pizza more than I like pizza, **or** does it mean she likes pizza more than she likes me? Well, it most likely means she likes pizza more than I like pizza, so say it correctly:

She likes pizza more than I do. (or She likes pizza more than I.)

7.3 Dangling and Misplaced Modifiers

Take a look at these sentences:

1. **While still in diapers, my mother** graduated from college.
2. The poet read from his **new book wearing glasses**.
3. **Sitting on bed of rice, I** thought the chicken looked delicious.
4. The girl walked her **dog in a bikini.**

The above sentences should make you laugh. This type of mistake is common and easy to make, but the sentences come out either unclear or downright ridiculous! The problem is that the participle is sitting next to the wrong word, thus implying that it modifies that word—or even modifying something that isn't even in the sentence.

1. The first sentence says that **my mother graduated from college while she was still in diapers.** Obviously, this is not what the writer intended; my mother graduated from college while *I* was still in diapers. However, the word ***mother*** is placed right next to ***while still in diapers.*** When words are next to each other, it is assumed that they go with each other. *I* isn't even in the sentence; therefore, the participle here is called **dangling.**

   Correct: *My mother graduated from college while I was still in diapers,* **OR**
   While I was still in diapers, my mother graduated from college.

2. Was the poet wearing glasses, or was the book wearing glasses? The sentence says that the new book was wearing glasses, but we know that is not the case. Make the sentence clearer. Put the ***wearing glasses*** phrase next to who was really wearing glasses!

   Correct: *Wearing glasses, the poet read from his book,* **OR**
   The poet wore glasses while he read from his book.

   (There are usually several ways to correct a sentence, so there are other options for fixing this sentence.)

3. Who or what was sitting on a bed of rice? Obviously, it was the chicken. However, this sentence says that *I* was!

   Correct: *Sitting on a bed of rice, the chicken looked delicious* is one way of fixing this sentence.

4. Who was wearing the bikini? Well, sometimes dogs do wear fancy outfits, but it was most likely the girl who was wearing the bikini!

   Correct: *The girl wearing the bikini was walking her dog,* **OR**
   The girl, wearing a bikini, was walking her dog, **OR**
   While wearing a bikini, the girl was walking her dog.

Note: The best way to avoid misplaced modifiers is to be careful and to always proofread your writing!

7.4 Possessives

Possessives show ownership. Only nouns and pronouns can be possessive. Generally, to form a possessive noun, we add an ***apostrophe*** and an ***s***.

Sarah's ball fell behind the sofa.

*The **boy's** toy is lost.*

To make a plural noun possessive, you usually just add an apostrophe after the *s*.

*The **boys'** toys were lost.* (More than one boy's toys)

*The **houses'** holiday lights were off.* (More than one house)

When a plural does not end in *s*, add an **apostrophe** and an *s* for the possessive.

*The **children's** toys were all broken.* (***Children*** is already plural without an *s*.)

A **singular** word that ends in *s* will generally have an **apostrophe** and an *s* added to make it possessive.

James's *essay was very good.* (The two *s*'s in a row might look odd, but notice how you pronounce ***James's***; you pronounce it just the way it is spelled. You do not pronounce it ***James'***.)

Think about how you would pronounce a word when deciding whether or not to add an apostrophe and an *s* to a word that already has an *s* at the end. For example, *princesses* is a plural word. To make it possessive, you would simply add an apostrophe. You would not say *princesses's* gowns. You would say *princesses'* gowns (pronounced exactly the same way as the plain plural *princesses*). For the singular possessive you would write (and say) *princess's*. Actually, the singular and plural possessives would be pronounced the same, although spelled differently (*princess's* and *princesses'*.)

Helpful Hints! Do not use an apostrophe to make a noun plural! The plural of *boy* is *boys*, not *boy's* (*boy's* is singular possessive). That goes for all nouns. The only time you use an apostrophe to make a word plural is for letters (*a*'s), numbers (*4*'s), symbols (*&*'s), and words used as themselves (for example: You have too many *and*'s in that sentence). Although a word used as itself is *italicized*, the *apostrophe* and the *s* are not.

Possessive pronouns do not have apostrophes: *The book is **ours**. The toy is **theirs**. This dress is **yours**. I know **its** name. **Whose** book is that?*

7.5 Active and Passive Voices

We talked a little about active and passive voice back in Chapter 1.3. **Voice** applies to verbs only.

To review, in **active voice** the subject of the verb is the thing or person doing the action of the verb. In **passive voice** the action of the verb is being done by someone or something other than the subject (in passive voice the "doer" of the verb may or may not be mentioned in the sentence).

Active voice: *I **am swimming** today.*
          *The **boy drove** the car to school today.*
          *The **dogs ran away** yesterday.*

Passive voice: *The **boy was driven** to school. (The boy* is the subject, but he did not do the driving.)
          *The **school was built** in the 1900s. (The school* is the subject, but it didn't build anything.)

The lesson here is to use the active voice most of the time in your writing. It is much stronger. We generally use the passive voice in these cases:

- You don't **know** who did it. (*The fire was set in the bathroom.*)
- You don't really **care** who did it. (*Audrey was awarded the gold medal.* The focus here is on Audrey getting the medal, not who gave it to her.)

7.6 *However* and *Therefore*

These two words are often punctuated incorrectly. Each of these two words can be used as an interrupter in the middle of a sentence. Each word can also be used at the beginning of a sentence—or after a semicolon—as a transition word.

Interrupter: *The book, however, is not in the library.* (You could leave out *however,* and the sentence would still make perfect sense, and it would not be a run-on.)

Transition Word: *I couldn't find the book. However, I think the library has it.* (Here, there are two separate sentences: *I couldn't find the book* is a sentence; *I think the library has it* is also a sentence. Therefore, you need a period or a semicolon between them. You **cannot** use just a comma instead of the period or semicolon; you would have a run-on sentence. Use an uppercase *H* after the period, but a lowercase *h* if you use a semicolon. Either way, *however* is generally followed by a comma.)

Interrupter: I won't have the book with me, *therefore,* to help me. (You could easily leave out *therefore.*)

Transition Word: I won't have the book; *therefore,* I will use another book. (There are two separate sentences here, so you need a semicolon or a period. You cannot use a comma instead of the semicolon; you would have a run-on sentence.)

Note: If *however* or *therefore* is in the middle of a sentence, try taking it out of the sentence. If you have a complete sentence left, put commas around *however* or *therefore.* If you have two sentences you need to use a period, a semicolon, or add a conjunction with the comma if it makes sense.

7.7 Using Strong Verbs

Your writing will be more lively and to the point if you choose your verbs carefully. With strong and precise verbs, you will need fewer adverbs. Better writing uses strong verbs and fewer adverbs. An important thing to remember is to not overuse forms of the verb *to be*: *are, is, have been, am, was.*

> **Weak and wordy:** There will be a meeting of the dance committee on Friday.

> **Better:** The dance committee will meet on Friday (shorter and more to the point).

> **Weak:** It is really nice out today.

> **Better:** The sun is shining today. (more descriptive)

Note: Remember that forms of the *to be* verb are often used as helping verbs with a main verb. It is fine to use those verbs (such as *are, am, will be, has been,* etc.) as helping verbs with another verb (for example, *is shining,* in the example above).

Helpful Hint! Avoid using *there is* (or *there was,* or *there will be,* etc.) to begin a sentence. It is a very weak construction.

7.8 Verb Tense Consistency

The twelve common verb tenses were discussed in Chapter 1.3, as well as some suggestions for using them correctly. Let us repeat here.

Avoid mixing tenses needlessly. Stay consistent!

> **Incorrect:**   *I **went** to her house, and she **gives** me some cookies* (needless switch from present to past tense).

> **Correct:**   *I **went** to her house, and she **gave** me some cookies.*

If you begin telling a story in past tense, don't suddenly switch to present tense. Things that happen at the same time should be expressed in the same tense. Of course, if you are speaking or writing in present tense and want to say something about an incident that happened in the past, switch to a past tense.

Also remember that when you talk or write about a book or a movie, you generally use present tense, rather than past, because the book or movie still exists.

7.9 Irregular Verb Forms

An irregular verb is a verb that does not add **-ed** or **-d** for past tense and past participle. The problem is that the English language has tons of irregular verbs that just need to be memorized. Here is a regular verb:

I walk   *I walked*   *I have walked*

Here are some of the more common problematic irregular verbs. This is by no means a complete list!

Present	Past	Past Participle
I buy	Yesterday, I bought	Every day, I have bought
I bring	Yesterday, I brought	Every day, I have brought
It bursts	Yesterday, it burst	Every day, it has burst
It costs	Yesterday, it cost	Every day, it has cost
I drag	Yesterday, I dragged	Every day, I have dragged
I drink	Yesterday, I drank	Every day, I have drunk
I freeze	Yesterday, I froze	Every day, I have frozen
I go	Yesterday, I went	Every day, I have gone
I hang	Yesterday, I hung	Every day, I have hung (a picture)
I hang	Yesterday, I hanged	Every day, I have hanged (a person)
I lay	Yesterday, I laid	Every day, I have laid
I lead	Yesterday, I led	Every day, I have led
I lend	Yesterday, I lent	Every day, I have lent
I lie	Yesterday, I lay	Every day, I have lain
I ring	Yesterday, I rang	Every day, I have rung
I rise	Yesterday, I rose	Every day, I have risen
I run	Yesterday, I ran	Every day, I have run
I set	Yesterday, I set	Every day, I have set
I shrink	Yesterday, I shrank	Every day, I have shrunk
I sit	Yesterday, I sat	Every day, I have sat

I sneak	Yesterday, I sneaked	Every day, I have sneaked
I speak	Yesterday, I spoke	Every day, I have spoken
I swim	Yesterday, I swam	Every day, I have swum
I swing	Yesterday, I swung	Every day, I have swung
I throw	Yesterday, I threw	Every day, I have thrown
I wake	Yesterday, I woke	Every day, I have woken
I wear	Yesterday, I wore	Every day, I have worn
I write	Yesterday, I wrote	Every day, I have written

Helpful Hint! Please note that *brang* and *broughten* are not words; and as weird as it might sound, *I have swum* and *I have drunk* are indeed correct. *I have went* should be *I have gone*; and you may *have hanged* a man, but you have *hung* curtains!

7.10 Linking Verbs and Pronouns

Just a little review here . . .

In Chapter 1.3 we discussed verbs, in Chapter 2.4 we discussed predicate words, and then in Chapter 6.10, we talked about when to use *I* and when to use *me*. When you use a **linking** verb, as opposed to an **action** verb, you use the subjective pronoun forms *I, he, she, they, we,* or *who* after the verb (rather than *me, him, her, them, us,* or *whom*). The pronoun after the linking verb is a **predicate nominative** and is in the subjective case.

Therefore, as weird as it sounds, *It is I* is correct, not *It is me*. Likewise, *It is she*, not *It is her*.

7.11 Parallel Structure

Parallel structure refers to the repetition of a grammatical pattern in a sentence. You should always use parallel structure in your writing.

It is best understood by example.

Not Parallel: I like to swim, to ski, and hunting.

Parallel: I like to swim, to ski, and to hunt.

Not parallel: He is kind, honest, and a good student. (*Kind* and *honest* are adjectives, so *a good student* should be made into an adjective; or you can make *kind* and *honest* parallel with *a good student*.)

Parallel: He is kind, honest, and conscientious.

Parallel: He is a kind boy, an honest citizen, and a good student.

Use parallel structure in lists as well.

Not Parallel:

This book explains
- How to power up your computer.
- How to begin the program.
- Using the printer.

Parallel:

This book explains
- How to power up your computer.
- How to begin the program.
- How to use the printer.

Make sure you use parallel structure in an *either/or* or *neither/nor* construction too.

Not parallel: He is neither athletic nor likes music.

Parallel: He is neither athletic nor musical.

7.12 Series and Lists

Horizontal Lists

If you have a series in a sentence, remember to use a comma after each item in the series and optionally, after the last item in the series (the Oxford comma).

The recipe calls for sugar, flour, cocoa, butter(,) and eggs.

Use a colon to introduce a series in a sentence **when the sentence ends before the series begins.**

> *I have these items in my purse: comb, pen, wallet, and keys.* (Here, there is a complete sentence before the series. The series does not complete the sentence.)

Do not use a colon to introduce a series in a sentence when the items are the ending part of the sentence.

> *In my purse I have a comb, a pen, a wallet, and keys.* (You would not put a colon after ***have*** because it would cut the sentence in half.)

Vertical Lists

Note that the words *follow* or *following* often, but not always, precede a vertical list.

For vertical lists, use a colon after the introductory sentence. You do not need to capitalize the items in the list (unless they are complete sentences, in which case you would begin each one with a capital letter).

I have the following items in my wallet:
- pen
- comb
- wallet
- keys

Make sure you do the following tasks:
- Clean the kitchen.
- Water the plants.
- Vacuum the rugs.
- Get the mail.

If the items in the list complete the introductory sentence, do not use a colon.

In my purse I have
- a pen
- a comb
- a wallet
- keys

Note: Make sure that your list items are parallel. If one item is a sentence, they should all be sentences. If they are phrases or sentences, they should all be structured in the same way.

7.13 Keeping It Simple

When a journalist writes a newspaper article, it needs to fit in the allotted space, so the editor will sometimes chop out the unnecessary words. Much of what we write is too wordy and can be slimmed down. Do not think that using big words and using lots of them improves your writing. It makes it more difficult to understand. Your writing goal (and speaking goal) is to be easily understood without sounding like a first grader.

Wordy: *He is a man who is very successful.*

Better: *He is successful.*

Wordy: *There will be a meeting held in the auditorium by the dance committee on Friday morning.*

Better: *The dance committee will meet in the auditorium Friday morning.*

Here are a few other wordy phrases:

The reason is because . . .

What I mean is . . .

Well, here's the thing . . .

It happens that . . .

7.14 Restrictive and Nonrestrictive Clauses

We talked about clauses in Chapter 2.6 and again in our discussion of commas in Chapter 3.2.

To review . . . a clause is a group of words with a subject and a verb. Independent clauses are complete sentences; this discussion is about dependent (or subordinate) clauses.

A **restrictive** clause is necessary for the meaning of the sentence and does not have commas around it. A **nonrestrictive** clause is added information and is set off with commas. These clauses are also called essential (restrictive) and nonessential (nonrestrictive).

Restrictive adjective clauses:

*The boy **who is sitting in the front seat** is my cousin.* (which boy?)

*The **book that is on the table** is due at the library.* (which book?)

Nonrestrictive adjective clauses:

*That boy, **who is my cousin,** will be playing violin in the show.*

*I love this dress, **which is on sale next week.***

Adverb clauses are generally restrictive. When they begin the sentence, they are followed by a comma because they are also introductory information. However, when they end the sentence, they are generally not preceded by a comma.

***Because I love this dress,** I will buy it.*

*I will buy this dress **because I love it.***

***After I finish baking them**, we can eat the cookies.*

*We can eat the cookies **after I finish baking them.***

> Proofread carefully to see if you any words out.
> —*Author Unknown*

Chapter 8

Questions You Might Have

This chapter answers some questions you still might have about grammar and writing style.

8.1 How Do I Capitalize Titles?

Here are the standards for capitalizing words in titles (book titles, movie titles, short story titles, song titles, chapter titles, etc.), headlines, and headings. Note that other styles exist, so if you are following a specific style guide, check there.

1. Capitalize the first and last words of a title no matter what they are.

2. Capitalize both parts of any hyphenated words.

3. Do **not** capitalize the following words unless they are the first or last word of a title:

Do not capitalize the articles *a, an,* or *the.*

Do not capitalize the FANBOYS conjunctions (*for, and, nor, but, or, yet, so*). However, if *yet* or *so* is being used as an adverb, do capitalize it.

Do not capitalize prepositions unless they are longer than three letters. (**Do not** capitalize short prepositions such as *at, in, out, for, up, to*; but **do** capitalize longer prepositions such as *with, above, below, between, among*.) If you see a word that looks like a preposition, but it is not in a prepositional phrase, it is being used as an adverb, so capitalize it. For example, "*out the door*" is a prepositional phrase, and *out* is the preposition. In "*I am going out*," *out* is not part of a prepositional phrase, so it is an adverb and should be capitalized.

Helpful Hint! Remember that although it is short, the word *is* is a verb and should always be capitalized in a title! That also applies to other forms such as *are, will be, were, was*, etc.

Let's assume these are book titles:

So Near Yet So Far Away (So is an adverb here; *yet* is a conjunction, but looks funny as the only lowercase word in the title, so I would capitalize it here. However, you don't need to.)

I Am Going Out Tonight (Although *out* can be a preposition, here it is not part of a prepositional phrase—for example, *out the door*—so it is being used as an adverb and should be capitalized.)

What Is Going On? (**Is** is a verb and is always capitalized in a title.)

8.2 Can I Use Abbreviations?

In general avoid using abbreviations in formal writing. In memos, lists, charts, and more technical writing, it is fine to use some abbreviations. Obviously, some words are usually abbreviated no matter what: *Dr., Mr., Ms., Jr.*

Many abbreviations do not have a period after them, for example, *ft* (foot), *mg* (milligram), *oz* (ounce), *lb* (pound), *gm* (gram), and *yd* (yard).

However, *in.* (inch) is followed by a period, so that it is not confused with the preposition *in*.

While we are talking about abbreviations, notice that many of those with all capital letters have no periods within them.

FBI, TV, CIA, USA, YMCA

Inc. (incorporated), *co.* (company), and *corp.* (corporation) are followed by a period. When you write company names, however, abbreviate and punctuate them the same way the company does—even if you don't agree with it.

Do not use abbreviations such as *e.g.*, *i.e.*, or *etc.*, in formal writing. Use the spelled out versions. Here they are:

etc. (*et cetera*) means "and so on" or "and all the rest." Try to put all the items in the list and avoid using *etc.*

Preferred: *I brought shoes, a hat, a coat, a scarf, and long underwear.*

Avoid: *I brought shoes, a hat, a coat, etc.*

i.e. means "that is," so simply say *that is.*

Preferred: *I used my good china, that is, the china my grandmother gave me.*

Avoid: *I used my good china, i.e., the china my grandmother gave me.*

e.g. means "for example," so just say "for example."

Preferred: *Take some winter clothes, for example, a hat, to the mountains.*

Avoid: *Take some winter clothes, e.g., a hat, to the mountains.*

Remember that *etc.*, *e.g.*, and *i.e.* are always both preceded and followed by a comma when you do use them in text.

8.3 Can I Use Contractions?

I tend to avoid using most contractions in formal writing. Formal writing means an essay or a business letter, as opposed to perhaps a story or a memo.

In formal writing, use *I am* instead of *I'm, you are* instead of *you're, he is* instead of *he's*. It is fine to use the occasional contraction. But I would avoid using contractions like *could've* for *could have* and other similar "shortcuts."

8.4 When Do I Spell Out Numbers?

Spelling out numbers depends on the type of writing you are doing. In scientific or technical writing, spell out numbers *one* through *nine*. Use numerals (for example, *15*) for numbers ten and higher. However, in literary writing, or when writing something scholarly in the humanities, numbers through *ninety-nine* are usually spelled out. Note that numbers from *twenty-one* through *ninety-nine* are hyphenated when they are two words.

In charts, figures, and tables, it is fine to use numerals for all your numbers. In fact, it looks much better in such cases if you handle all numbers the same way.

If you have a sentence with two related numbers and one is over ten (or over 99) and one under, treat them the same way.

The class consisted of 8 boys and 16 girls.

There are eight parts of speech and about five hundred comma rules!

Never begin a sentence with a numeral.

One hundred boys were waiting in line.

Even in a chart or table, instead of a series of zeroes, you can spell out numbers such as *3 million or three million.*

Dimensions, sizes, and exact temperatures are always expressed in numerals. For example, *She wears a size 12 dress.*

With a.m. or p.m. always use numbers: *Please meet me at 8 p.m.*

With o'clock you can use either words or numbers: *It is three o'clock; it is 3 o'clock.*

Fractions, such as two-thirds, are hyphenated.

8.5 Can I Start a Sentence with a Conjunction?

In formal writing, do not start a sentence with a FANBOYS conjunction. These conjunctions include *for, and, nor, but, or, yet*, and *so*. If you are using more of a conversational tone (like the one in this book), you can occasionally start a sentence with a conjunction for effect—if it makes sense.

You can, however, begin a sentence with a **subordinating** conjunction such as *because, although, if, whenever*, and *since*. Just make sure that the adverb clause the conjunction introduces is followed by a complete sentence:

Correct: *Because I have no money, I cannot go to the movies with you.*

Incorrect: *Because I have no money.* (not a complete sentence)

Correct: *If you clean your room, you can go out to play.*

Incorrect: *If you clean your room.* (not a complete sentence)

8.6 Can I Ever Use Fragments and Run-Ons?

A sentence fragment, to review, is a group of words that does not make a complete sentence. In informal writing, you can use fragments, sparingly, to create an effect or to make a point. Advertisements are full of sentence fragments. But, promise me that you won't use a fragment because you thought it was a complete sentence! You can break the rules only when you know them.

Here are some samples of writing using fragments. Fragments are in bold:

I never met a dog I didn't like. **Never.** *If I could, I would have a house full of dogs.*

There are eight parts of speech in the English language. **Remember: eight.**

A run-on consists of two (or more) sentences that are not correctly separated. Usually we separate our sentences with periods. We can also use a semicolon if the two sentences are closely related in meaning. Another way of avoiding a run-on is to use a comma and a FANBOYS conjunction. Usually run-ons are separated incorrectly with a comma only (also called a **comma splice**).

Run-on: I received your letter, I am sorry it took me so long to reply.

Fix #1: I received your letter. I am sorry it took me so long to reply.

Fix #2: I received your letter; I am sorry it took me so long to reply.

Fix #3: I received your letter, and I am sorry it took me so long to reply.

So, can you use run ons? NO. NEVER.

8.7 Can I Use Jargon and Slang?

Wassup, dude? **Slang** has no place in most writing! The only place I can think of it being appropriate is in dialog in a novel. Obviously, you can speak to your friends using slang, but in formal writing or speech, no.

Jargon is generally thought of as the specific language of a particular occupation or interest. There is medical jargon, technical jargon, grammar jargon (yes!), baseball jargon, legal jargon, and the list goes on. If you are writing or speaking to an audience consisting of a group of lawyers, you are free to use the jargon they will understand. Likewise, if you are writing to doctors or tekkies, you can use medical terms or tech terms that your audience is familiar with.

8.8 And Last . . . A Few Common Mistakes

This section consists of some random questions and mistakes that frequently come up.

1. **I couldn't care less** is correct. **I could care less** is incorrect.
2. **Different from** is correct. **Different than** is incorrect.
3. **Moot point** is correct. **Mute point** is incorrect.
4. **A whole nother** is a common way to say **another whole**, but **a whole nother** is incorrect.

5. The saying is **taken aback**, not **taken back**.

6. **With regard to** is correct, not **with regards to** when we are referring to something.

7. **Based on** is correct, not **based off**.

8. You **figuratively** hit the ceiling, not **literally**. **Literally** means you really did hit the ceiling.

9. You graduated **from high school**; you didn't **graduate high school**.

10. **My teacher gave us a test** is correct. **My teacher he gave us a test** is incorrect.

Final Test

1. Which of these is a prepositional phrase?
   a. is a dog   b. anyone who sees   c. and me   d. for my birthday

2. Which of these is a coordinating conjunction?
   a. too   b. whom   c. because   d. but

3. Every sentence needs a subject and a(n) _____
   a. verb   b. noun   c. object   d. period

4. *After dinner I will play the piano.* The subject of this sentence is
   a. dinner   b. piano   c. I   d. play

5. Which of the following is a pronoun?
   a. I   b. Jack   c. man   d. anyway

6. **Give the book to Steve.** What type of sentence is this?
   a. interrogative   b. imperative   c. exclamatory   d. statement

7. Which of these phrases contains a participle?
   a. to be a teacher   b. diving is fun   c. up the stairs
   d. frozen food

8. Which sentence has a participle that makes sense?
   a. Driving down the road, my dog chased me.
   b. He read from his book wearing glasses.
   c. Reading a book by the window, my cat fell asleep.
   d. Running down the street, she tripped and fell.

9. An independent clause is the same as a(n)
   a. phrase   b. subordinate   c. infinitive   d. sentence

10. Which one of the following is a clause?
    a. after I watch the movie
    b. running down the street
    c. Jack and Jill
    d. before the game

11. Which of these is a sentence fragment?
    a. Because I can't go with you.
    b. Going to the movies with my mother and brother is fun.
    c. She ran.
    d. She ran, he walked.

12. Which one of these is a run-on sentence?
    a. I told you, but you didn't listen.
    b. She ran; he walked.
    c. I didn't go, he did.
    d. Give me the book, put the games away, wash your face, and go to bed.

13. Which of these is a complex sentence?
    a. Jack and Jill went up the hill.
    b. Jack went up the hill because he liked to climb.
    c. Jack went up the hill, and Jill fell down.
    d. Jill climbed and climbed up the hill.

Each of these sentences has one mistake. Correct each sentence:

14. Give the books to Jeane and myself.

15. You should of given those candy bars to my sister and me.

16. With whom are you going.

17. Do you want these kind of pencils or the newer ones?

18. Anyone who is on the girl's soccer team can buy their uniform here.

19. Neither of my brother's is coming with us.

20. Either the dogs or the baby are making a mess.

21. Joe waved at his friend as he was walking down the street.

22. After she had swum three miles, she said she was alright.

23. I baked cookies this morning, would you like one?

24. I have drunk all the milk so I will go to the store to buy more.

25. If I was taller, I could probably be a model.

26. I had rung the bell five times, before she answered the door.

27. The dress, that I am holding, is on sale.

28. Jack, Ben, and I are going; but John, Frank, and him are not.

29. Did she ask "Can I go with you?"

30. My favorite song is *Summertime*.

31. This recipe needs: salt, sugar, flour, milk, three types of chocolate, and four eggs.

32. I read this quote by Mayor Geary: "These (the new taxes) will help pay for the roads to be fixed."

33. She attends Proctor High School, in Memphis, Tennessee.

34. She said that "the weather should be nice today."

35. The title of the movie is *Where is Mr. Jones?*

36. Dear Mister Duple,
    I am applying for the accounting position at Tickner, Inc.

37. Yours Truly,
    John Jones, Jr.

38. Jim, along with his friends, are going to see a concert.

39. He likes to swim more than me, but I am a better swimmer.

40. Finally repaired, I picked up my car from the shop today.

41. She asked me if I heard about the meeting in the restroom.

42. I would have gone to Thomas' house, but he is on vacation.

43. I met the following people at my interview: Ann Jones, the company president, the human resources manager; Phil Cole, a project manager; and a scientist.

44. Five boys and 20 girls are in the class.

45. You put too many a's in the word accommodate.

46. They almost stole 75 percent of my money!

47. After we hanged the pictures on the wall, the apartment looked really good.

48. Well, I didn't hardly want any cake anyway, did you?

49. After the storm the rocks were laying all over the road.

50. I am going to try to get a job in Sales.

See Appendix E for the answers.

Appendix A
Commonly Misspelled Words

These words are common—and commonly misspelled

Accidentally

Accommodate

Acquire

Believe

Calendar

Category

Cemetery

Changeable

Column

Committed

Conscience (the guilty kind)

Conscientious

Conscious (aware)

Definitely

Discipline

Embarrass

Existence

Foreign

Gauge

Guarantee

Harass

Humorous

Immediately

Inoculate

Intelligence

Jewelry

Judgment

Kernel (corn)
   (*Colonel* is the military rank.)

Leisure

Liaison

Library

License

Maintenance

Millennium

Minuscule

Mischievous

Misspell

Noticeable

Occasionally

Occurrence

Perseverance

Possession

Precede
  (to come before something else)

Proceed (to go ahead)

Privilege

Pronunciation

Questionnaire

Receive/Receipt

Recommend

Referred

Reference

Relevant

Restaurant

Rhyme

Rhythm

Schedule

Separate

Twelfth

Until

Vacuum

Weird

Appendix B
Commonly Mispronounced Words

The following words are often mispronounced.

Acrost–should be **across** (no **t** at the end)

Febyuary–should be *February* (don't forget the **r**)

Heighth–should be *height* (with a **t** sound at the end, not **th**)

Jewlery–should be *jewelry*

Liberry–should be *library* (don't forget the **r**)

Mischeevious–should be *mischievous* with the accent on the first syllable and the last syllable having a **vus** sound.

Perscription–should be **prescription**

Probly–should be *probably*

Pronounciation–should be *pronunciation*

Realator–should be **realtor**

Reoccur–should be *recur*

Supposably–should be *supposedly*

Undoubtably–should be *undoubtedly*

Appendix C
A Writing Lesson

Now that you know all the rules, as well as what you should avoid, it is time to write. Learning the rules doesn't do much good unless you apply them in your writing and speaking.

Above all, writing should be clear and easy to understand. We are not talking about writing the Great American Novel here—although that may be your goal, which is also fine. We are talking about things you might write at your job or at school, such as memos, letters, and reports.

You don't need to use big words, or a large number of words, to write well. However, your writing needs to be clear, well organized, and interesting. You can make your writing interesting by using descriptive verbs and a variety of sentence structures.

All writing needs a beginning, a middle, and an end.

Paragraphs

A paragraph is made up of several related sentences. Letters, reports, and essays are usually made up of several paragraphs, but sometimes you might write just one paragraph—for a memo perhaps. A paragraph needs an introductory sentence, called a **topic sentence**, to introduce your topic for the paragraph; all the other sentences in the paragraph hang on that topic sentence and should stick to the topic. If you are writing just one paragraph, you should also have a concluding sentence to wrap things up. Within your paragraphs, use transition words (***to begin***, ***next***, ***finally***, etc.), if necessary, to make your writing flow.

Here is a sample one-paragraph memo:

The planning committee will hold a meeting on Thursday at 9 a.m. in the main conference room on the first floor. Attendees should be prepared to discuss several issues at this meeting. We will begin with a review of the new building plans. Please bring your blueprints if you have them. Next, we will talk about the budget for the new construction. Finally, we would like to hear your opinions about the new recreation center on the 9th floor. We will be distributing a survey before the meeting. Please bring your survey to the meeting. We look forward to what we hope will be a productive morning!

In the above memo, there is an opening, or topic, sentence. The rest of the paragraph sticks to that topic (the meeting). The last sentence wraps it all up. The transition words ***begin***, ***next***, and ***finally*** are used to create flow between the ideas.

Note: In this book I have not indented paragraphs. Instead, I have skipped lines between paragraphs because the format was complex, and I thought it was easier to read that way. However, when you write, you should indent paragraphs. Do not skip lines between paragraphs when you indent.

Multi-Paragraph Writing

Whether you are writing an essay, a report, or a business letter, anything with multiple paragraphs follows a pattern: The opening paragraph tells the readers what you are going to tell them. The middle paragraph or paragraphs gives the readers the bulk of the information. The final paragraph, or conclusion, tells the readers what you just told them—and sometimes calls for some action to be taken.

The middle paragraphs are similar to the paragraphs we talked about in the previous section, when we discussed the structure of a paragraph. Each paragraph in a multi-paragraph writing (except the introduction and the conclusion) has a topic sentence, which tells what the paragraph is about. Every sentence in the paragraph sticks to that topic.

Here is an example of a multi-paragraph letter. It is a letter of complaint by a consumer who recently purchased a new refrigerator.

To whom it may concern:

Last month I purchased a refrigerator manufactured by your company. I bought it at ABC Appliance in Wonderville. The model number is 76400-3. I am writing to you at this time because I am very unhappy with the product for a couple of reasons. I am hoping you can do something to solve the problem.

To begin, immediately after the refrigerator was installed, it began making loud banging noises almost constantly. I called the repair number, and a repair person from your company took a look at it. Since it is under warranty, there was no charge. The repair person made some adjustments and told me the problem was fixed. Several hours later the banging noise began again. I have repeatedly called ABC Appliance, and they told me to call you.

In addition to the noise problem, the refrigerator does not keep food cool at a consistent temperature. Sometimes we find that our food has frozen in the refrigerator! Other times the food is hardly cold. All the members of my family have noticed this problem at different times.

Needless to say, I am very disappointed in the performance of this appliance. I do not have the confidence that it can be repaired. I would like to return the unit to the store for a full refund and buy another brand. I am hoping your company will authorize this refund.

Sincerely yours,

Joseph Smith

TOMAS: The Five Aspects of Good Writing:

T = Thought. Brainstorm to gather your thoughts.

O = Organization. Outline to make sure your thoughts are organized before you write.

M = Mechanics. Make sure your grammar, punctuation, spelling, and word usage is correct.

A = Audience. Know to whom you are writing. Writing to children is different from writing to computer professionals.

S = Develop your own style through practice.

Glossary

Here is a list of some common grammar terms:

Abstract noun A noun that you cannot see, hear, touch, taste, or smell. *Examples: happiness, thought*

Active voice Writing in which the subject of the sentence is performing the action of the verb. *Example: She drove the car.*

Adjective One of the eight parts of speech. An adjective describes a noun or another adjective and usually tells what kind or how many. *Examples: purple, pretty, seven*

Adverb One of the eight parts of speech. An adverb describes a verb, an adjective, or another adverb and usually tells how, when, or to what extent. *Examples: slowly, very, now*

Agreement The rule that says singular subjects go with singular verbs, plural subjects go with plural verbs, singular pronouns go with singular antecedents, and plural pronouns go with plural antecedents. *Example:* **Everyone** *should have* **his or her** *pencil.*

Antecedent The word (noun or pronoun) that a pronoun stands in for. *Example:* **Mary** *brought her book.*

Appositive A phrase that adds more information to a noun or pronoun. *Example: Ben,* **my older brother**, *is twelve years old.*

Article The words *a, an*, and **the**. They are actually adjectives.

Clause A group of words that has a subject and a verb. *Example: That book,* **which I read last night**, *is a mystery.*

Collective noun A noun that even in its singular form represents a group. *Examples: group, flock, bunch, herd*

Common noun A person, place, or thing that does not begin with a capital letter. *Examples: boy, dog, house, radio*

Comparative The adjective or adverb form that is used when comparing two things, generally the *-er* or ***more*** form. *Examples: **taller** of the two girls, **more fun** than the other game*

Complex sentence A sentence with one or more dependent clauses and one independent clause. *Example: Although I am tired, I will go with you.*

Compound sentence A sentence with two or more independent clauses. *Example: **I am tired,** but **I will go with you.***

Compound-complex sentence A sentence with one or more dependent clauses and two or more independent clauses. *Example: Although I am tired, I will go with you, and I will have fun!*

Concrete noun A person, place, or thing you can see, hear, feel, taste, and/or smell. *Examples: desk, teacher, computer*

Dash (– en, — em) The en dash is used for ranges of numbers and minus signs. The em dash is used for a break in a sentence.

Demonstrative pronoun The pronouns that are used to point out: ***this, that, these,*** and ***those***

Direct object A noun or pronoun that generally comes after the verb and receives its action. *Example: I threw the **ball**.*

Double negative The use of two negatives, which makes it a positive and is grammatically incorrect. *Examples: I **don't** have **no** paper. I am **not hardly** ready.*

Fragment A group of words that is intended to be a sentence, but instead is an incomplete thought. *Example: Because I said so.*

Gerund A verb form ending in *-ing* that is used as a noun rather than a verb. *Example: **Reading** is my favorite hobby.*

Indefinite pronoun Pronouns such as ***anyone, anything, anybody, everyone, everything, everybody, someone, something, someone, none, few,*** and ***all***. Most of these pronouns are singular.

Independent clause A sentence, or complete thought.

Indirect object Noun or pronoun that *receives* the direct object in a sentence. *Example: He gave **me** the map.*

Infinitive A verb preceded by the word ***to***. *Example: to run*

Intensive pronoun A pronoun that ends in *-**self*** or *-**selves*** and is used for emphasis. *Example: He **himself** made an appearance at the party.*

Interjection One of the eight parts of speech: a word that expresses emotion. *Example: ouch! wow! oh!*

Interrogative pronouns The pronouns that are used to ask questions: ***which, who, whom, whose***, and ***what***

Irregular verb A verb that does not form its past tense with the addition of *-ed*. *Examples: run (ran), see (saw), sit (sat)*

Italics *Tilted letters in print.* You cannot write in italics.

Linking verb A verb that functions as an equal sign in a sentence, where both sides of the verb are equal. The most common linking verb is ***to be** (**am, are, is**)*. *Example: He **is** a boy.*

Lowercase Another word for small letters, as opposed to capital letters (uppercase)

Noun One of the eight parts of speech: a person, place, thing, or idea. *Examples: car, dog, city, sofa, thought*

Objective case The pronoun forms that are used as direct and indirect objects, and objects of a preposition. They are ***me, us, her, him, them***, and ***whom***.

Participle A verb form, usually the past tense or *-**ing*** form, that is used as an adjective. *Example: I drove past the **burning** building.*

Passive voice Grammatical construction where the subject of the sentence is not performing the action of the verb. *Example: I was driven to school.*

Phrase A small group of related words that does not contain both a subject and a verb.

Possessive A form of a noun or pronoun that shows ownership. *Examples: hers, Susan's, the children's*

Predicate The simple predicate is the verb in the sentence. The complete predicate is the entire sentence except the subject.

Preposition One of the eight parts of speech. A preposition is always the first word in a prepositional phrase. The phrase usually tells where or when. *Examples: in the box, after the party*

Pronoun One of the eight parts of speech. A pronoun takes the place of a noun. *Examples: She, this, who, someone, I*

Proper noun A noun that names a particular person, place, thing, or idea and begins with a capital letter. *Examples: John, Texas, Pacific Ocean, Buddhism*

Punctuation marks The symbols that make text readable by telling the reader when to stop or pause. *Examples: periods, commas, colons, semicolons, quotation marks, dashes, hyphens, parentheses*

Reflexive pronoun A pronoun that ends in *-self* or *-selves* and is used to refer back to the same person in a sentence: *Example: **I** baked this pie **myself.***

Relative pronoun A pronoun that begins an adjective clause: ***that, which, who, whom,*** and ***whose***. *Examples: This is the dress **that** I just bought. My neighbor, **who** lives next door, is from Italy.*

Run-on sentence Two sentences with either no punctuation or a comma separating them. There needs to be either a period or semicolon separating them, or a conjunction added after the comma. *Example: The flower is pink, it is very pretty.* This is incorrect.

Simple sentence A sentence that consists of just one independent clause. *Example: Jack and I went to the movies.*

Subject Noun or pronoun that the sentence is about. The subject generally performs the action of the verb. *Examples: **She** saw the art exhibit. The **dog** bit the young child.*

Subordinate clause (dependent) A clause (group of words with a subject and a verb) that is not a complete thought and cannot stand alone as a sentence. *Example: although I received my driver's license*

Superlative The adjective or adverb form that is used when comparing more than two things, generally the *-est* or ***most*** form. *Examples: **tallest** of all the girls, **the most fun** of the three games*

Tense Form of a verb that tells when the action was done. The most common tenses are past, present, and future. *Examples: I walk, I walked, I will walk*

Uppercase Another word for capital letters, as opposed to small letters (lowercase)

Verb One of the eight parts of speech. Every sentence needs at least one verb. Represents action or a state of being. *Examples: run, talk, cook, is, looks*

Voice Active or passive. Tells whether the subject performs the action of the verb or not. *Examples: She baked a cake (active voice). A cake was baked by her (passive voice).*

Appendix E
Final Test Answers

1. Which of these is a prepositional phrase?
   a. is a dog   b. anyone who sees   c. and me   **d. for my birthday**

2. Which of these is a coordinating conjunction?
   a. too   b. whom   c. because   **d. but**

3. Every sentence needs a subject and a(n) _____
   a. verb   b. noun   c. object   d. period

4. *After dinner I will play the piano.* The subject of this sentence is
   a. dinner   b. piano   **c. I**   d. play

5. Which of the following is a pronoun?
   a. I   b. Jack   c. man   d. anyway

6. *Give the book to Steve.* What type of sentence is this?
   a. interrogative   **b. imperative**   c. exclamatory
   d. statement

7. Which of these phrases contains a participle?
   a. to be a teacher   b. diving is fun   c. up the stairs
   d. frozen food

8. Which sentence has a participle that makes sense?
   a. Driving down the road, my dog chased me.
   b. He read from his book wearing glasses.
   c. Reading a book by the window, my cat fell asleep.
   d. Running down the street, she tripped and fell.

9. An independent clause is the same as a(n)
   a. phrase   b. subordinate   c. infinitive   **d. sentence**

10. Which one of the following is a clause?
    a. after I watch the movie
    b. running down the street
    c. Jack and Jill
    d. before the game

11. Which of these is a sentence fragment?
    a. Because I can't go with you.
    b. Going to the movies with my mother and brother is fun.
    c. She ran.
    d. She ran, he walked.

12. Which one of these is a run-on sentence?
    a. I told you, but you didn't listen.
    b. She ran; he walked.
    c. I didn't go, he did.
    d. Give me the book, put the games away, wash your face, and go to bed.

13. Which of these is a complex sentence?
    a. Jack and Jill went up the hill.
    b. Jack went up the hill because he liked to climb.
    c. Jack went up the hill, and Jill fell down.
    d. Jill climbed and climbed up the hill.

Each of these sentences has one mistake. Correct each sentence:

14. Give the books to Jeane and **me.**

15. You should **have** given those candy bars to my sister and me.

16. With whom are you going**?**

17. Do you want **this** kind of pencils or the newer ones?

18. Anyone who is on the girl's soccer team can buy **her** uniform here.

19. Neither of my **brothers** is coming with us.

20. Either the dogs or the baby **is** making a mess.

21. **As Joe was walking down the street, he waved at his friend.**

22. After she had swum three miles, she said she was **all right.**

23. I baked cookies this morning; would you like one? (or use a period)

24. I have drunk all the milk, so I will go to the store to buy more.

25. If I **were** taller, I could probably be a model.

26. I had rung the bell five times before she answered the door.
    (omit comma)

27. The dress that I am holding is on sale. (omit commas)

28. Jack, Ben, and I are going; but John, Frank, and **he** are not.

29. Did she ask, "Can I go with you?"

30. My favorite song is **"Summertime."** (quotes instead of italics)

31. This recipe needs salt, sugar, flour, milk, three types of chocolate,
    and four eggs. (omit colon)

32. I read this quote by Mayor Geary: "These **[the new taxes]** will help
    pay for the roads to be fixed."

33. She attends Proctor High School in Memphis, Tennessee.
    (omit first comma)

34. She said that the weather should be nice today.
    (omit quotation marks)

35. The title of the movie is *Where **Is** Mr. Jones?*

36. Dear Mister Duple**:**
    I am applying for the accounting position at Tickner, Inc.

37. Yours **truly,**
    John Jones, Jr.

38. Jim, along with his friends, **is** going to see a concert.

39. He likes to swim more than **I,** but I am a better swimmer.

40. **Because it was finally repaired,** I picked up my car from the
    shop today. (There are other ways to fix the misplaced modifier.)

41. **In the restroom** she asked me if I heard about the meeting.

42. I would have gone to **Thomas's** house, but he is on vacation.

43. I met the following people at my interview: Ann Jones, the company president; the human resources manager; Phil Cole, a project manager; and a scientist.

44. Five boys and **twenty** girls are in the class.

45. You put too many ***a*'s** in the word accommodate.
    (italicize only the *a*)

46. They **stole almost** 75 percent of my money!

47. After we **hung** the pictures on the wall, the apartment looked really good.

48. Well, I **didn't want** any cake anyway, did you?

49. After the storm the rocks were **lying** all over the road.

50. I am going to try to get a job in **sales.**

Index

Contact and Ordering Information

We appreciate comments and questions sent to **info@bigwords101.com**.

We also appreciate **Amazon reviews** about this book and our other grammar books.

Check out and sign up for the **Grammar Diva Blog** at
http://bigwords101.com/category/blog/
Check out the website at **www.bigwords101.com**.

All the Grammar Diva's books are available in **PDF format** from the website. They are also available from **Amazon and all other online retailers**. E-books are available for **Kindle and all other e-book readers**.

If you would like to order bulk quantities of any of our books, contact **Ingram Distributors** for print books or the **iBook store** for e-books.

And, finally, all our print books are available **to order at any bookstore**.

The Grammar Diva is available for

- **grammar talks and presentations**
- **grammar workshops**
- **copyediting and writing**

Arlene Miller

THE GRAMMAR DIVA

Made in the USA
Middletown, DE
24 January 2020

83695285R00080